THE DARK TOWER
~THE GUNSLINGER~

THE JOURNEY BEGINS

CREATIVE DIRECTOR AND EXECUTIVE DIRECTOR
STEPHEN KING

PLOTTING AND CONSULTATION
ROBIN FURTH

SCRIPT
PETER DAVID

ART
SEAN PHILLIPS AND RICHARD ISANOVE

LETTERING
VC'S RUS WOOTEN

GALLERY 13
New York   London   Toronto   Sydney   New Delhi

Gallery 13
An Imprint of Simon & Schuster, Inc.
1230 Avenue of the Americas
New York, NY 10020

This book is a work of fiction. Any references to historical events, real people, or real places are used fictitiously. Other names, characters, places, and events are products of the authors' imagination, and any resemblance to actual events or places or persons, living or dead, is entirely coincidental.

Contains material originally published in magazine form by Marvel Comics as *Stephen King's The Dark Tower: The Gunslinger—The Journey Begins* #1-5

First Gallery 13 hardcover edition February 2019

For information about special discounts for bulk purchases, please contact Simon & Schuster Special Sales at 1-866-506-1949 or business@simonandschuster.com.

The Simon & Schuster Speakers Bureau can bring authors to your live event. For more information or to book an event, contact the Simon & Schuster Speakers Bureau at 1-866-248-3049 or visit our website at www.simonspeakers.com.

Manufactured in the United States of America

2 4 6 8 10 9 7 5 3 1

Library of Congress Cataloging-in-Publication Data is available.

ISBN 978-1-9821-0984-4
ISBN 978-1-9821-0985-1 (ebook)

In a world that has moved on...

Roland Deschain is the last descendant in the line of Arthur Eld. His late father, Steven, was the king of the barony of Gilead. Goaded by his father's enemies and seeking to emulate his patriarch, Roland was the youngest man to ever earn the title of "gunslinger." Great forces have swirled around him since that day. When Gilead was under attack by the armies of evil, led by "the Good Man" John Farson, Steven Deschain was killed, and his forces of the White known as the Affiliation faltered in their defense of the city. Roland and his *ku-tet* of gunslingers became Gilead's final barrier, and they, too, failed.

For nigh unto ten years, Roland, the lone survivor of that last, losing battle, has pursued his destiny—to reach the mysterious Dark Tower, the nexus of all realities, wherein he can set this out-of-sync world right. And the key to his goal lies with the sorcerous Man in Black, whom Roland now doggedly tracks. . . .

STEPHEN KING

THE DARK TOWER
~ THE GUNSLINGER ~

THE JOURNEY BEGINS
CHAPTER ONE

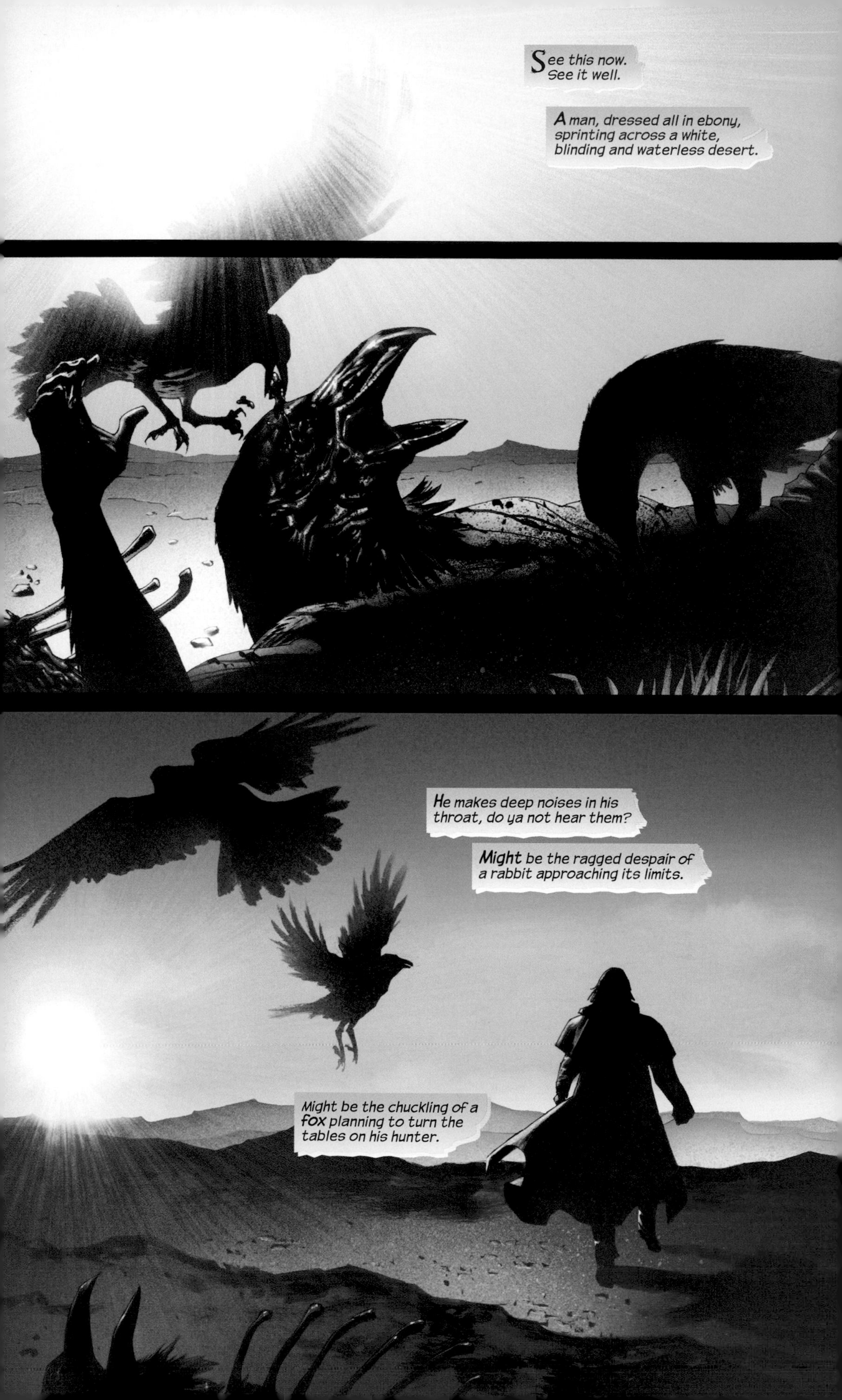
See this now. See it well.
A man, dressed all in ebony, sprinting across a white, blinding and waterless desert.
He makes deep noises in his throat, do ya not hear them?
Might be the ragged despair of a rabbit approaching its limits.
Might be the chuckling of a fox planning to turn the tables on his hunter.

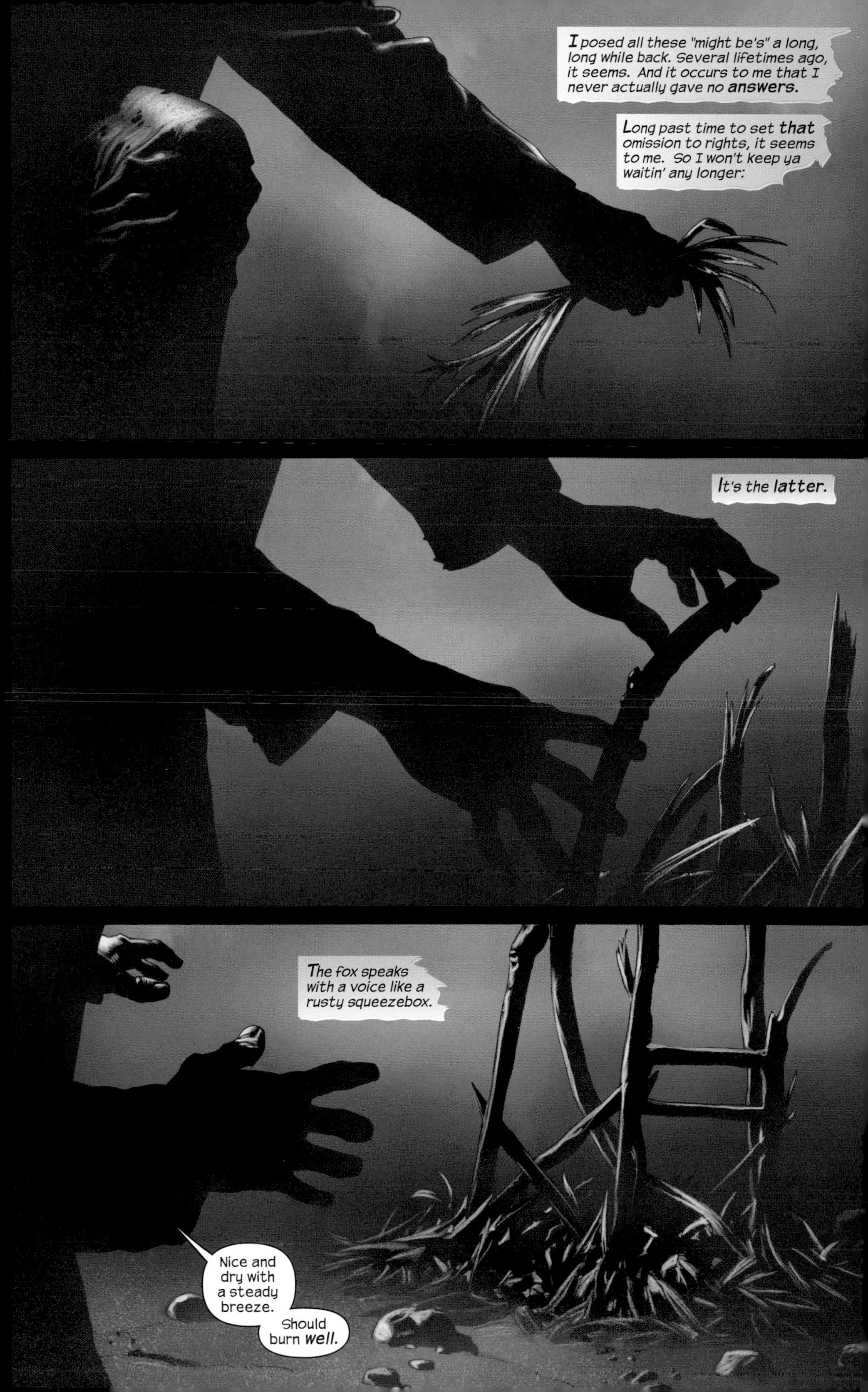

I posed all these "might be's" a long, long while back. Several lifetimes ago, it seems. And it occurs to me that I never actually gave no answers.
Long past time to set that omission to rights, it seems to me. So I won't keep ya waitin' any longer:
It's the latter.
The fox speaks with a voice like a rusty squeezebox.
Nice and dry with a steady breeze.
Should burn well.

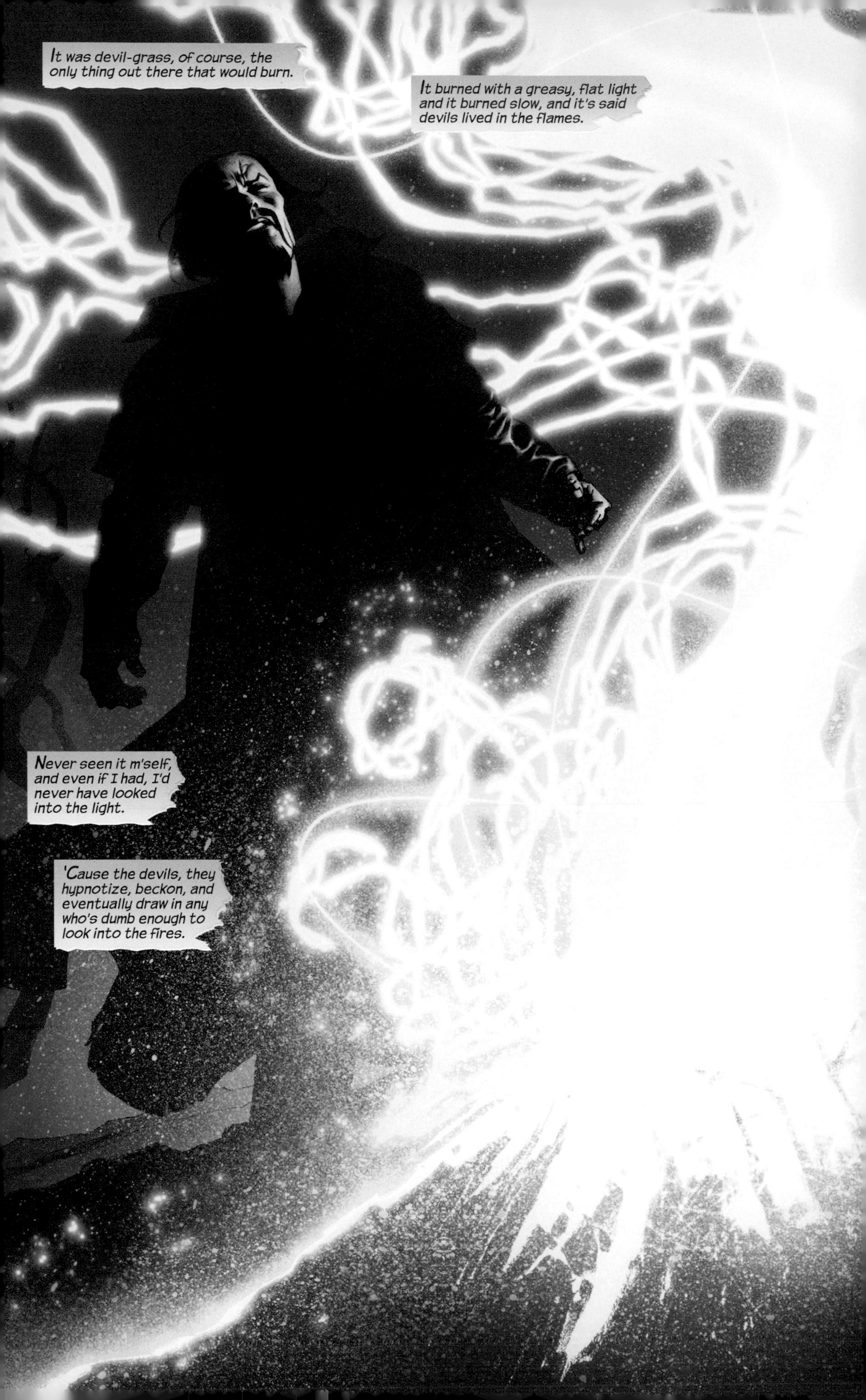
It was devil-grass, of course, the only thing out there that would burn.
It burned with a greasy, flat light and it burned slow, and it's said devils lived in the flames.
Never seen it m'self, and even if I had, I'd never have looked into the light.
'Cause the devils, they hypnotize, beckon, and eventually draw in any who's dumb enough to look into the fires.

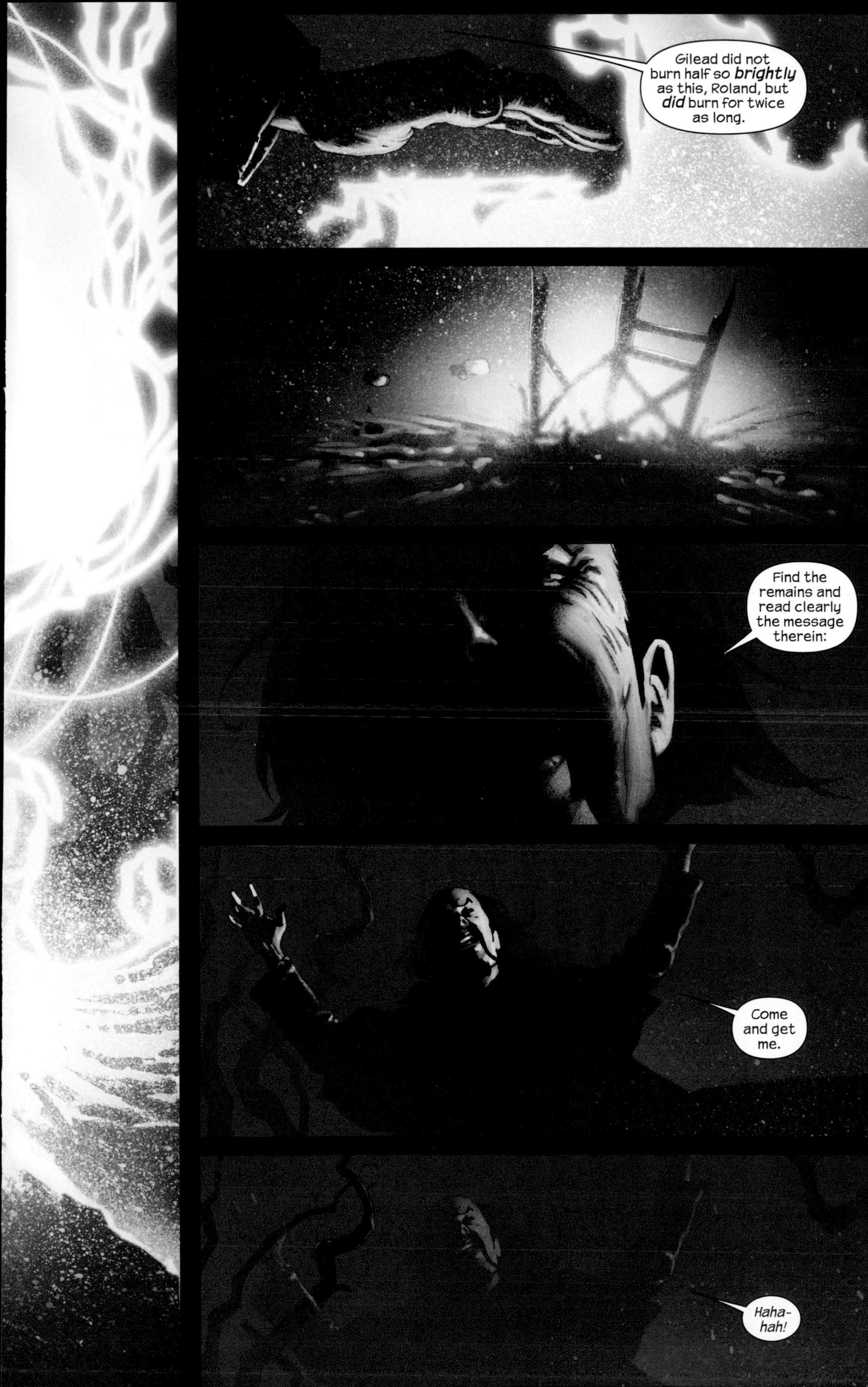
Gilead did not burn half so *brightly* as this, Roland, but *did* burn for twice as long.
Find the remains and read clearly the message therein:
Come and get me.
Haha-hah!

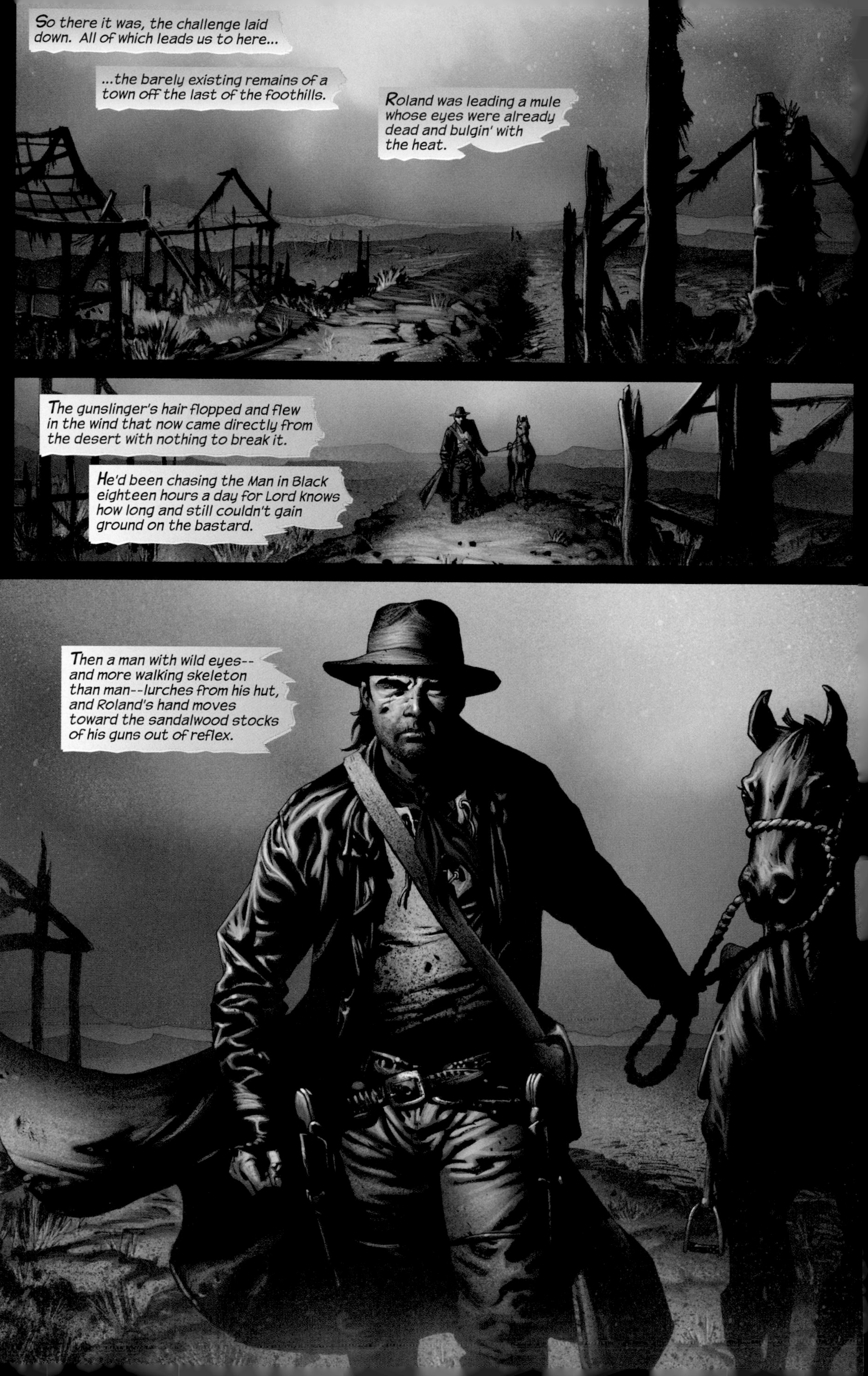
So there it was, the challenge laid down. All of which leads us to here...
...the barely existing remains of a town off the last of the foothills.
Roland was leading a mule whose eyes were already dead and bulgin' with the heat.
The gunslinger's hair flopped and flew in the wind that now came directly from the desert with nothing to break it.
He'd been chasing the Man in Black eighteen hours a day for Lord knows how long and still couldn't gain ground on the bastard.
Then a man with wild eyes--and more walking skeleton than man--lurches from his hut, and Roland's hand moves toward the sandalwood stocks of his guns out of reflex.

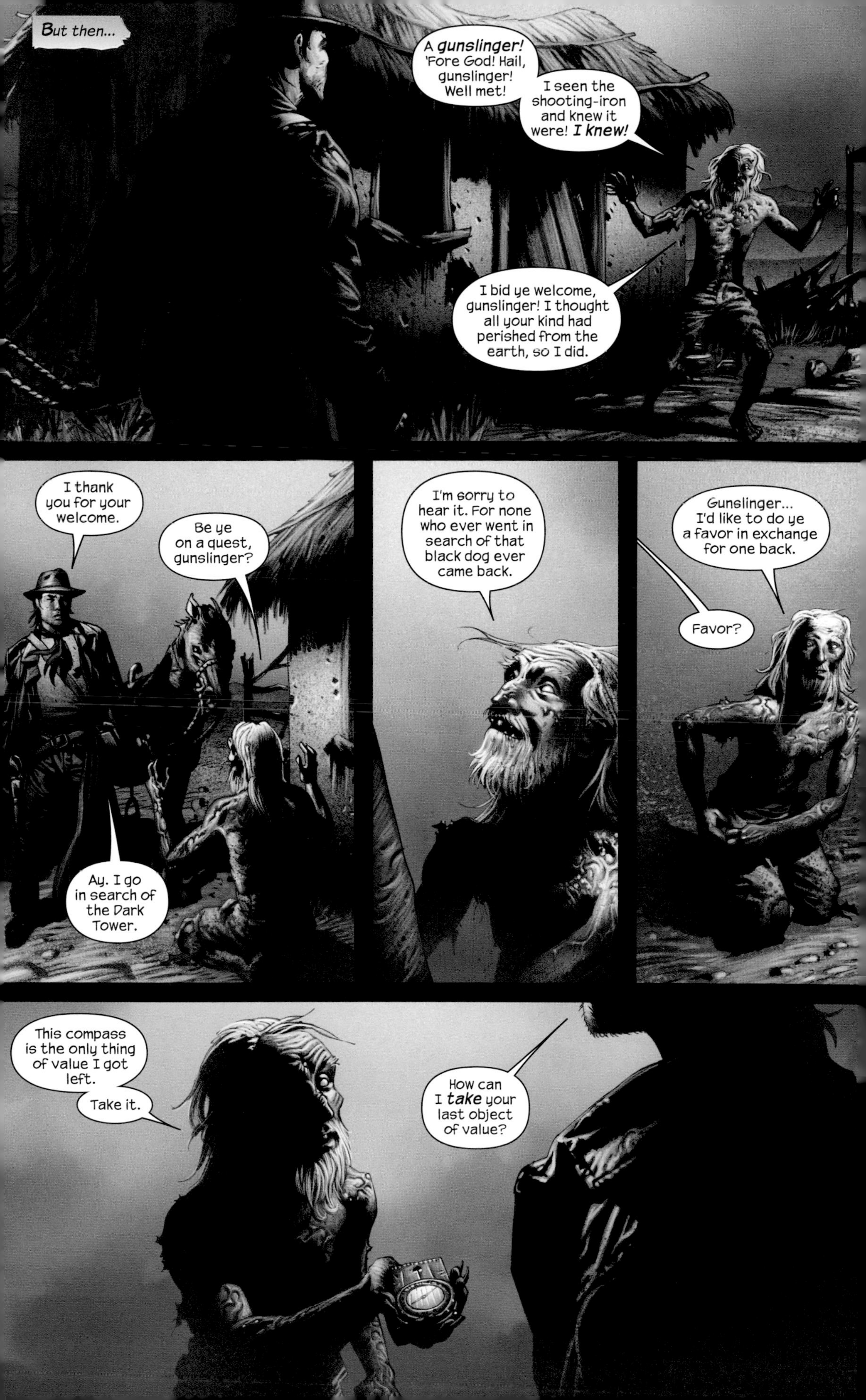

But then...
A gunslinger! 'Fore God! Hail, gunslinger! Well met!
I seen the shooting-iron and knew it were! I knew!
I bid ye welcome, gunslinger! I thought all your kind had perished from the earth, so I did.
I thank you for your welcome.
Be ye on a quest, gunslinger?
Ay. I go in search of the Dark Tower.
I'm sorry to hear it. For none who ever went in search of that black dog ever came back.
Gunslinger... I'd like to do ye a favor in exchange for one back.
Favor?
This compass is the only thing of value I got left.
Take it.
How can I take your last object of value?

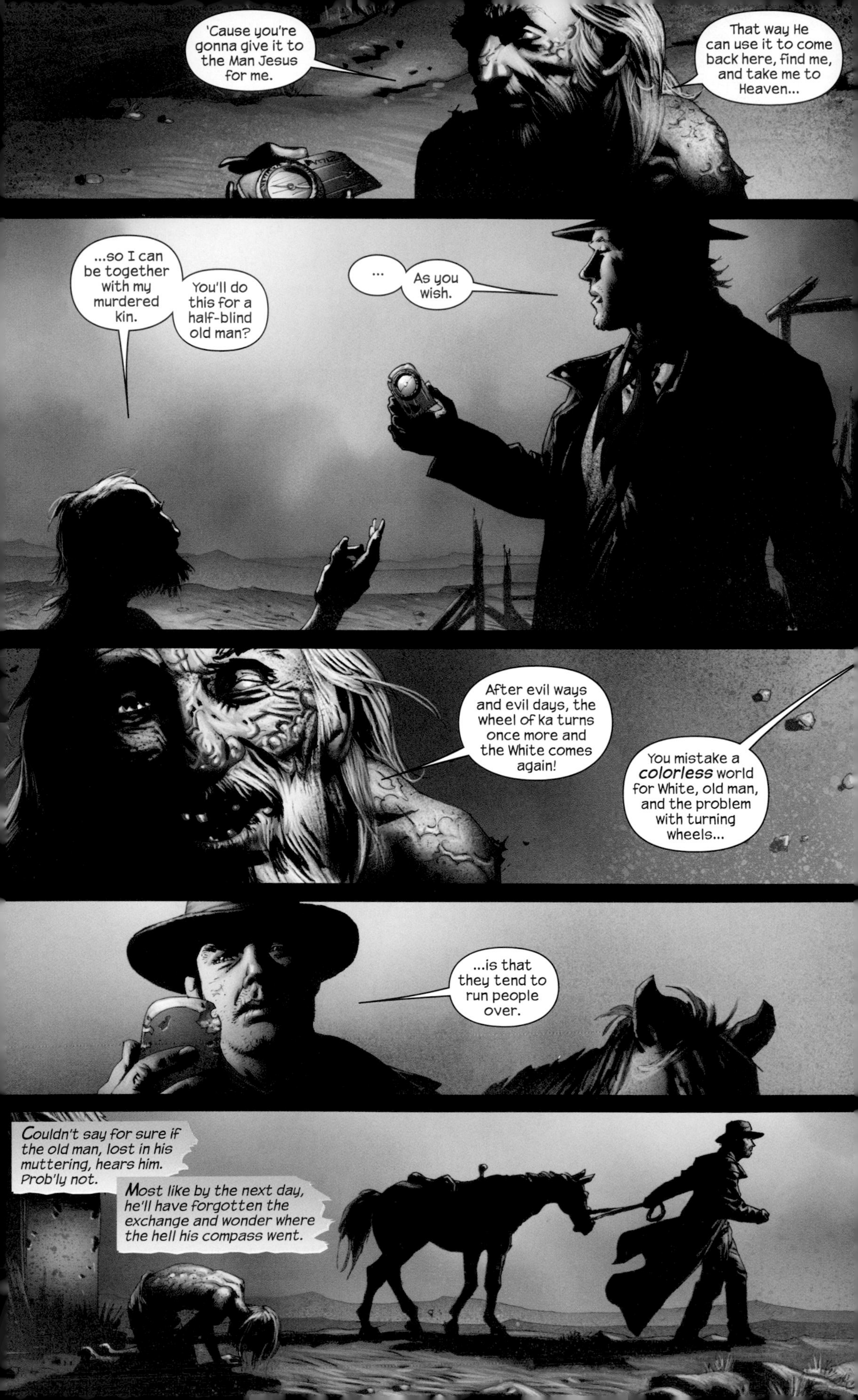
'Cause you're gonna give it to the Man Jesus for me.
That way He can use it to come back here, find me, and take me to Heaven...
...so I can be together with my murdered kin.
You'll do this for a half-blind old man?
...
As you wish.
After evil ways and evil days, the wheel of ka turns once more and the White comes again!
You mistake a *colorless* world for White, old man, and the problem with turning wheels...
...is that they tend to run people over.
Couldn't say for sure if the old man, lost in his muttering, hears him. Prob'ly not.
Most like by the next day, he'll have forgotten the exchange and wonder where the hell his compass went.

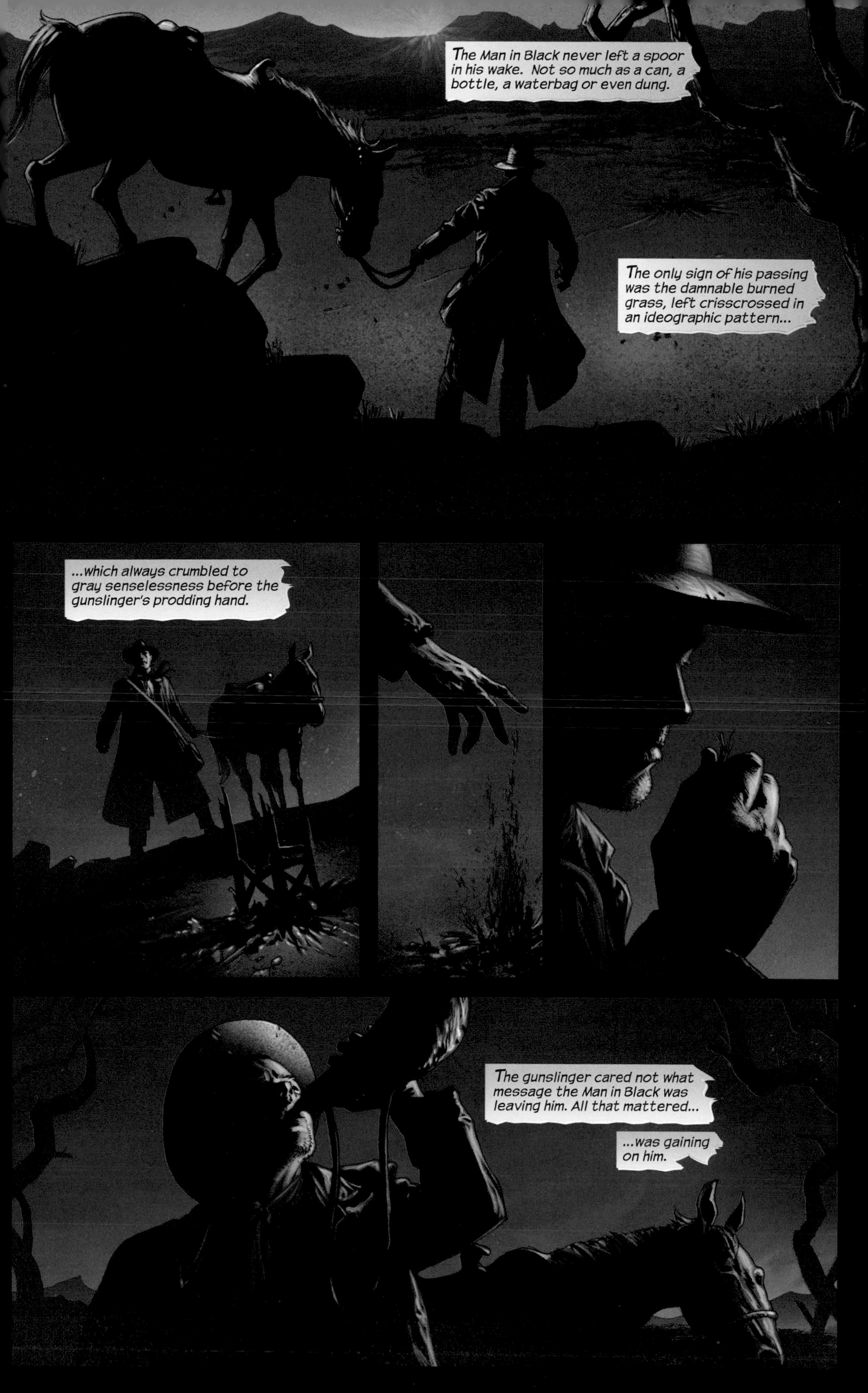
The Man in Black never left a spoor in his wake. Not so much as a can, a bottle, a waterbag or even dung.
The only sign of his passing was the damnable burned grass, left crisscrossed in an ideographic pattern...
...which always crumbled to gray senselessness before the gunslinger's prodding hand.
The gunslinger cared not what message the Man in Black was leaving him. All that mattered...
...was gaining on him.

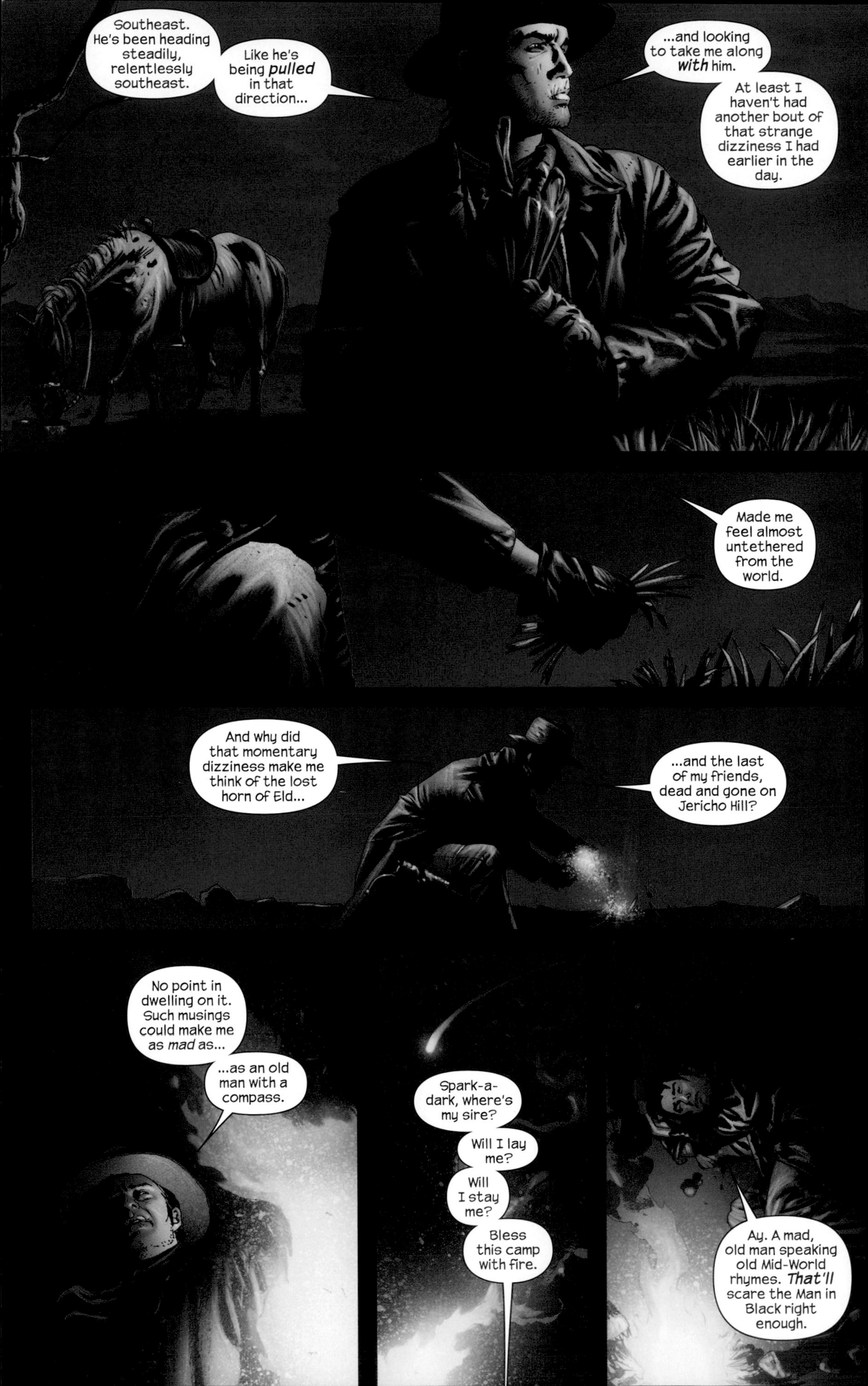
Southeast. He's been heading steadily, relentlessly southeast.
Like he's being *pulled* in that direction...
...and looking to take me along *with* him.
At least I haven't had another bout of that strange dizziness I had earlier in the day.
Made me feel almost untethered from the world.
And why did that momentary dizziness make me think of the lost horn of Eld...
...and the last of my friends, dead and gone on Jericho Hill?
No point in dwelling on it. Such musings could make me as *mad* as...
...as an old man with a compass.
Spark-a-dark, where's my sire?
Will I lay me?
Will I stay me?
Bless this camp with fire.
Ay. A mad, old man speaking old Mid-World rhymes. *That'll* scare the Man in Black right enough.

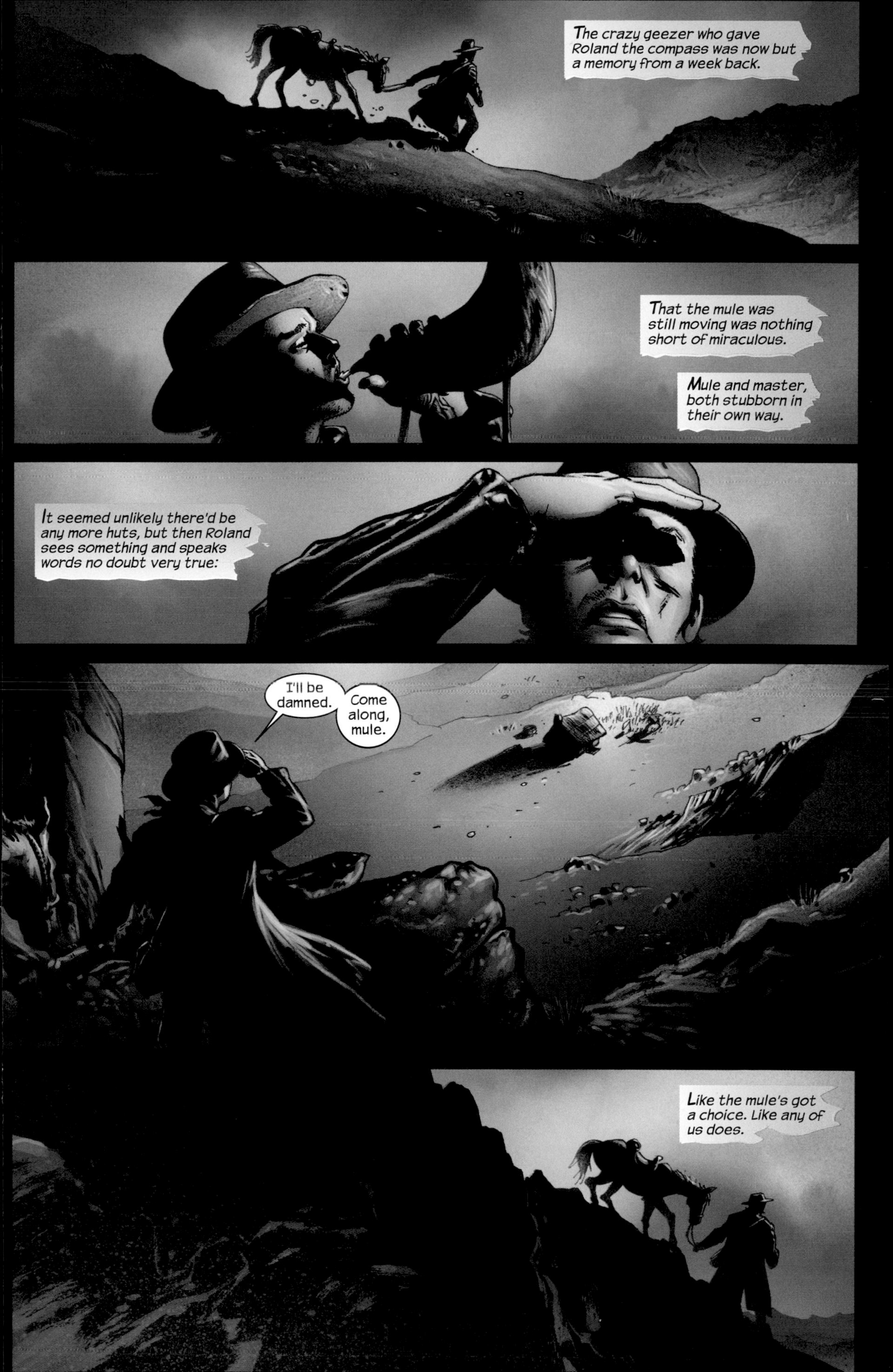
The crazy geezer who gave Roland the compass was now but a memory from a week back.
That the mule was still moving was nothing short of miraculous.
Mule and master, both stubborn in their own way.
It seemed unlikely there'd be any more huts, but then Roland sees something and speaks words no doubt very true:
I'll be damned.
Come along, mule.
Like the mule's got a choice. Like any of us does.

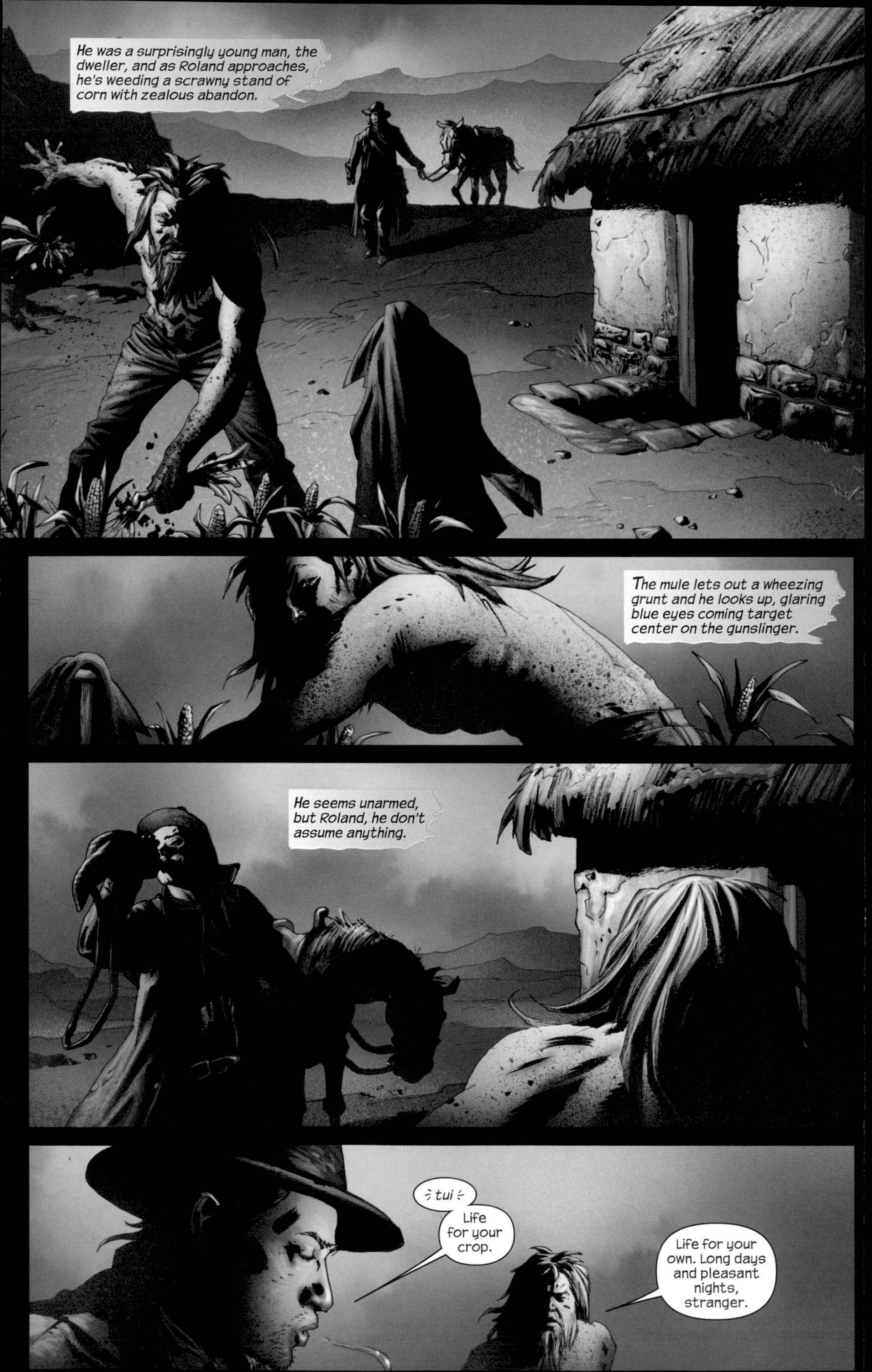
He was a surprisingly young man, the dweller, and as Roland approaches, he's weeding a scrawny stand of corn with zealous abandon.
The mule lets out a wheezing grunt and he looks up, glaring blue eyes coming target center on the gunslinger.
He seems unarmed, but Roland, he don't assume anything.
tui
Life for your crop.
Life for your own. Long days and pleasant nights, stranger.

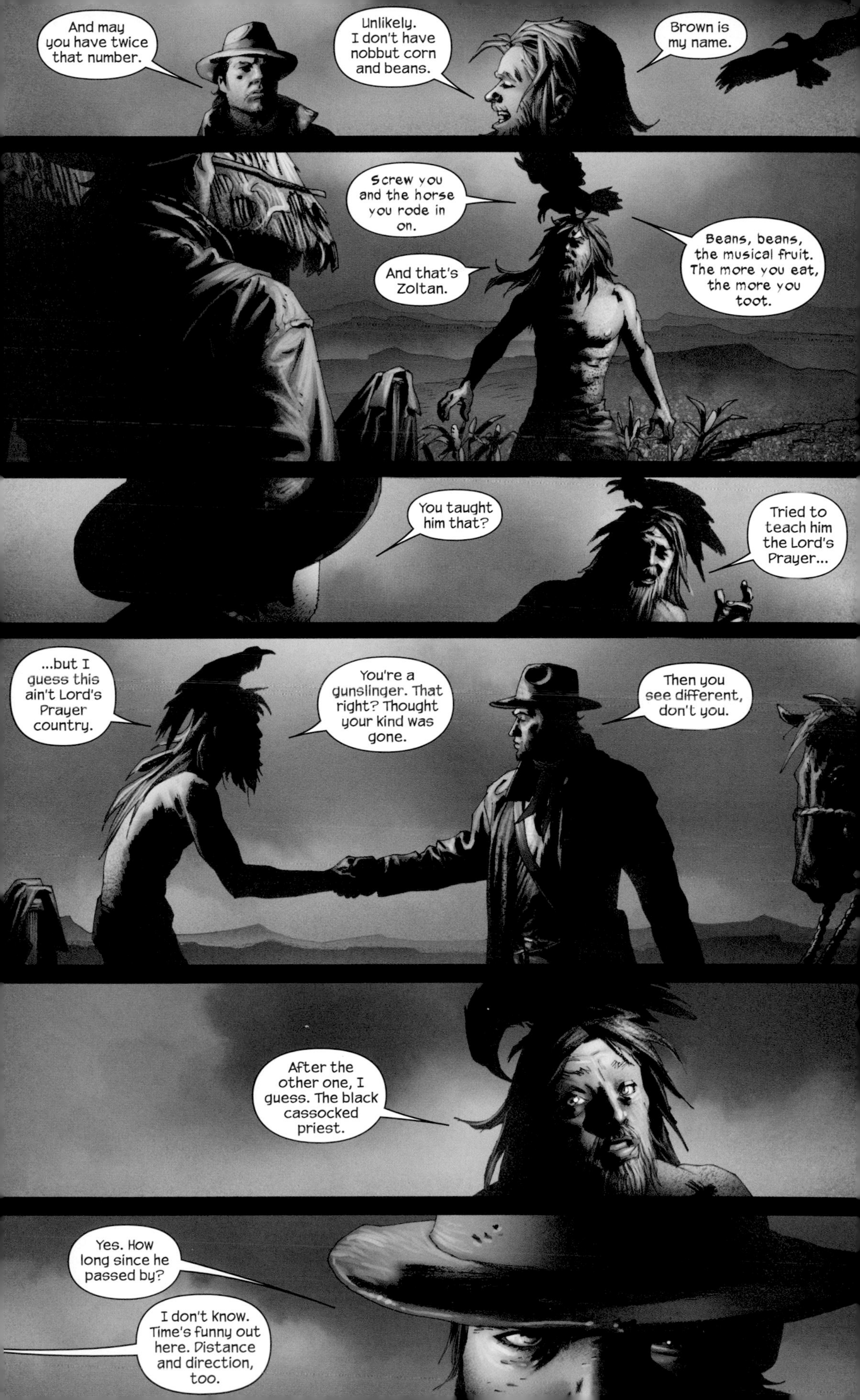
And may you have twice that number.
Unlikely. I don't have nobbut corn and beans.
Brown is my name.
Screw you and the horse you rode in on.
And that's Zoltan.
Beans, beans, the musical fruit. The more you eat, the more you toot.
You taught him that?
Tried to teach him the Lord's Prayer...
...but I guess this ain't Lord's Prayer country.
You're a gunslinger. That right? Thought your kind was gone.
Then you see different, don't you.
After the other one, I guess. The black cassocked priest.
Yes. How long since he passed by?
I don't know. Time's funny out here. Distance and direction, too.

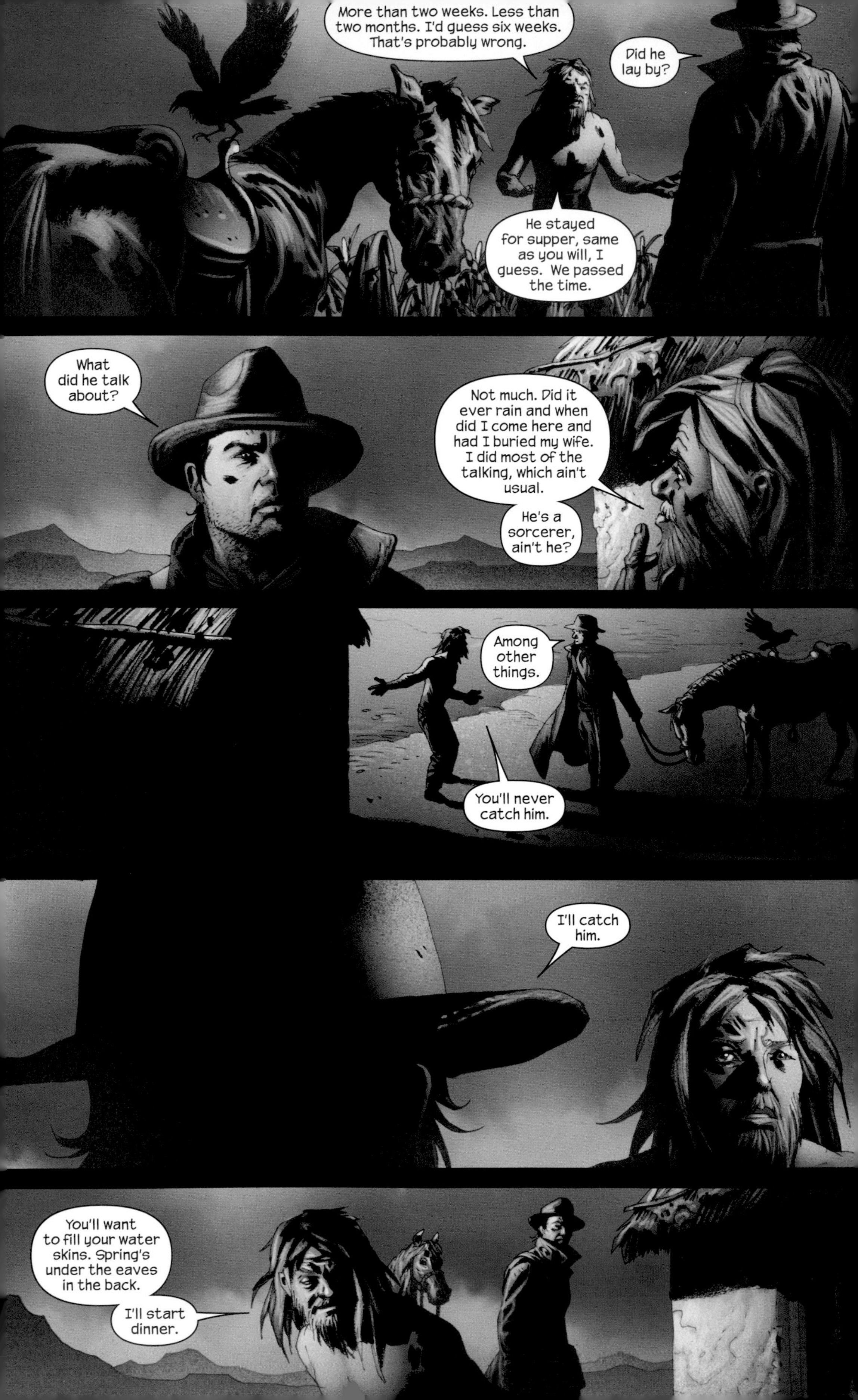
More than two weeks. Less than two months. I'd guess six weeks. That's probably wrong.
Did he lay by?
He stayed for supper, same as you will, I guess. We passed the time.
What did he talk about?
Not much. Did it ever rain and when did I come here and had I buried my wife. I did most of the talking, which ain't usual.
He's a sorcerer, ain't he?
Among other things.
You'll never catch him.
I'll catch him.
You'll want to fill your water skins. Spring's under the eaves in the back.
I'll start dinner.

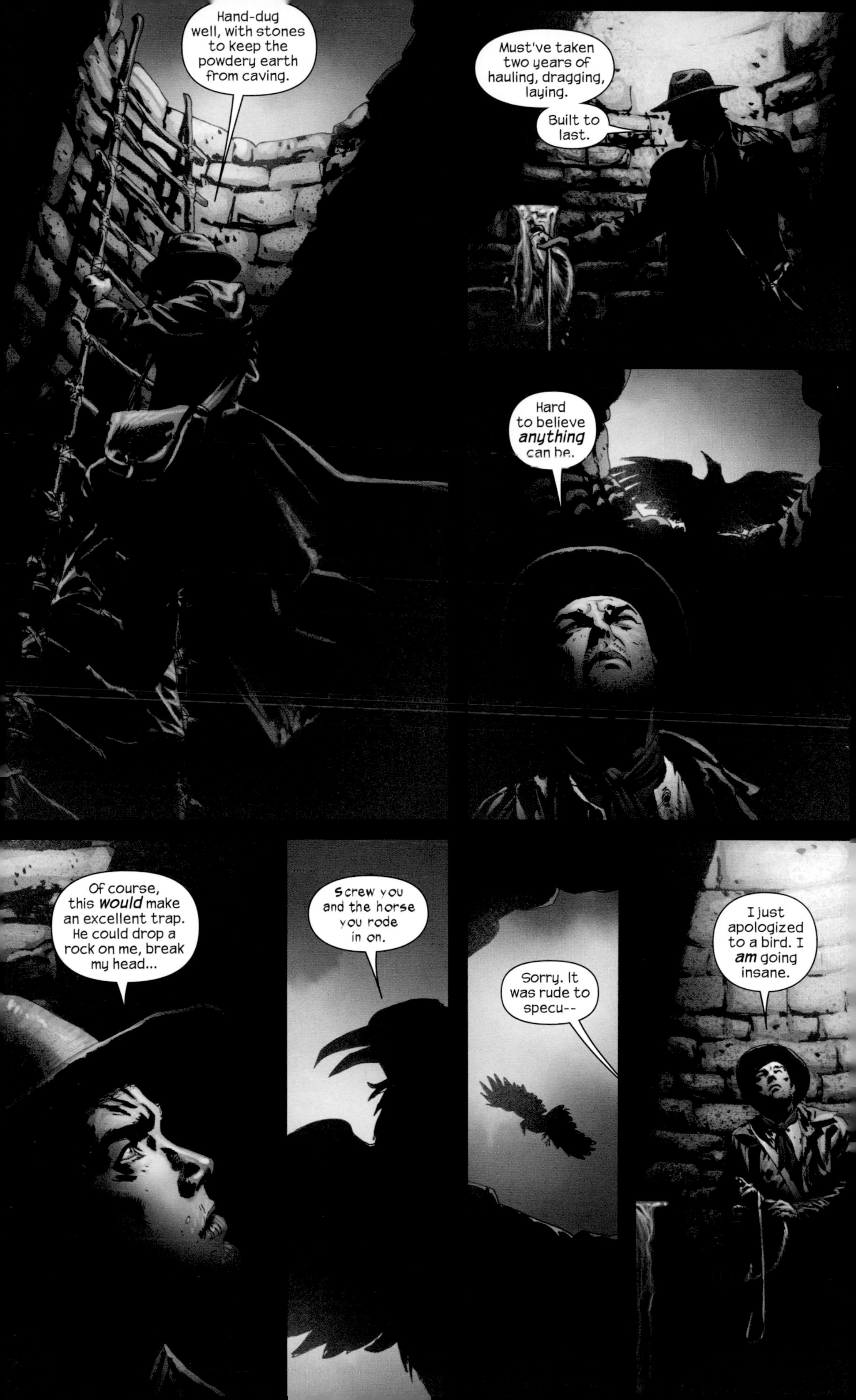
Hand-dug well, with stones to keep the powdery earth from caving.
Must've taken two years of hauling, dragging, laying.
Built to last.
Hard to believe *anything* can be.
Of course, this *would* make an excellent trap. He could drop a rock on me, break my head...
Screw you and the horse you rode in on.
Sorry. It was rude to specu--
I just apologized to a bird. I *am* going insane.

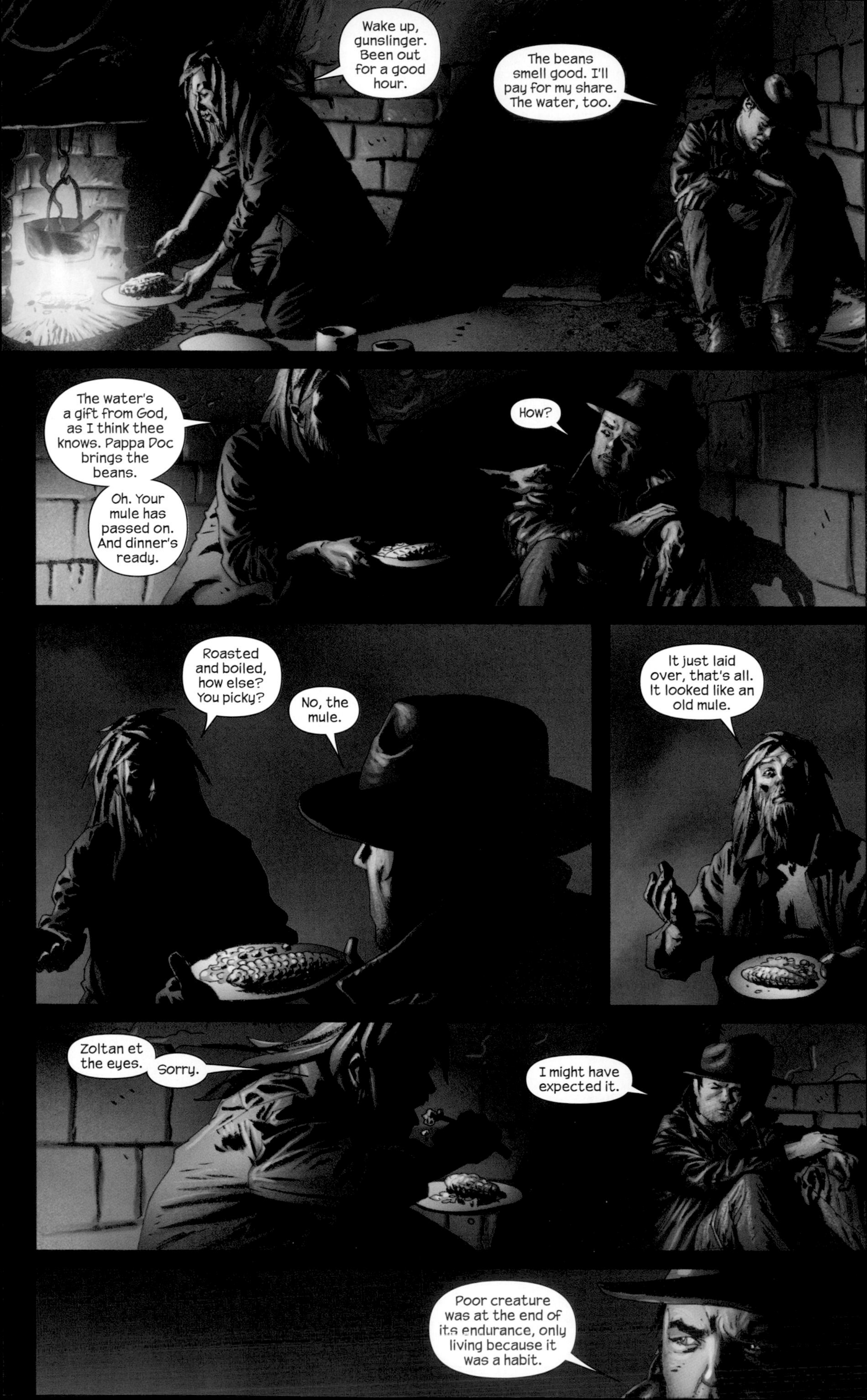
Wake up, gunslinger. Been out for a good hour.
The beans smell good. I'll pay for my share. The water, too.
The water's a gift from God, as I think thee knows. Pappa Doc brings the beans.
How?
Oh. Your mule has passed on. And dinner's ready.
Roasted and boiled, how else? You picky?
No, the mule.
It just laid over, that's all. It looked like an old mule.
Zoltan et the eyes.
Sorry.
I might have expected it.
Poor creature was at the end of its endurance, only living because it was a habit.

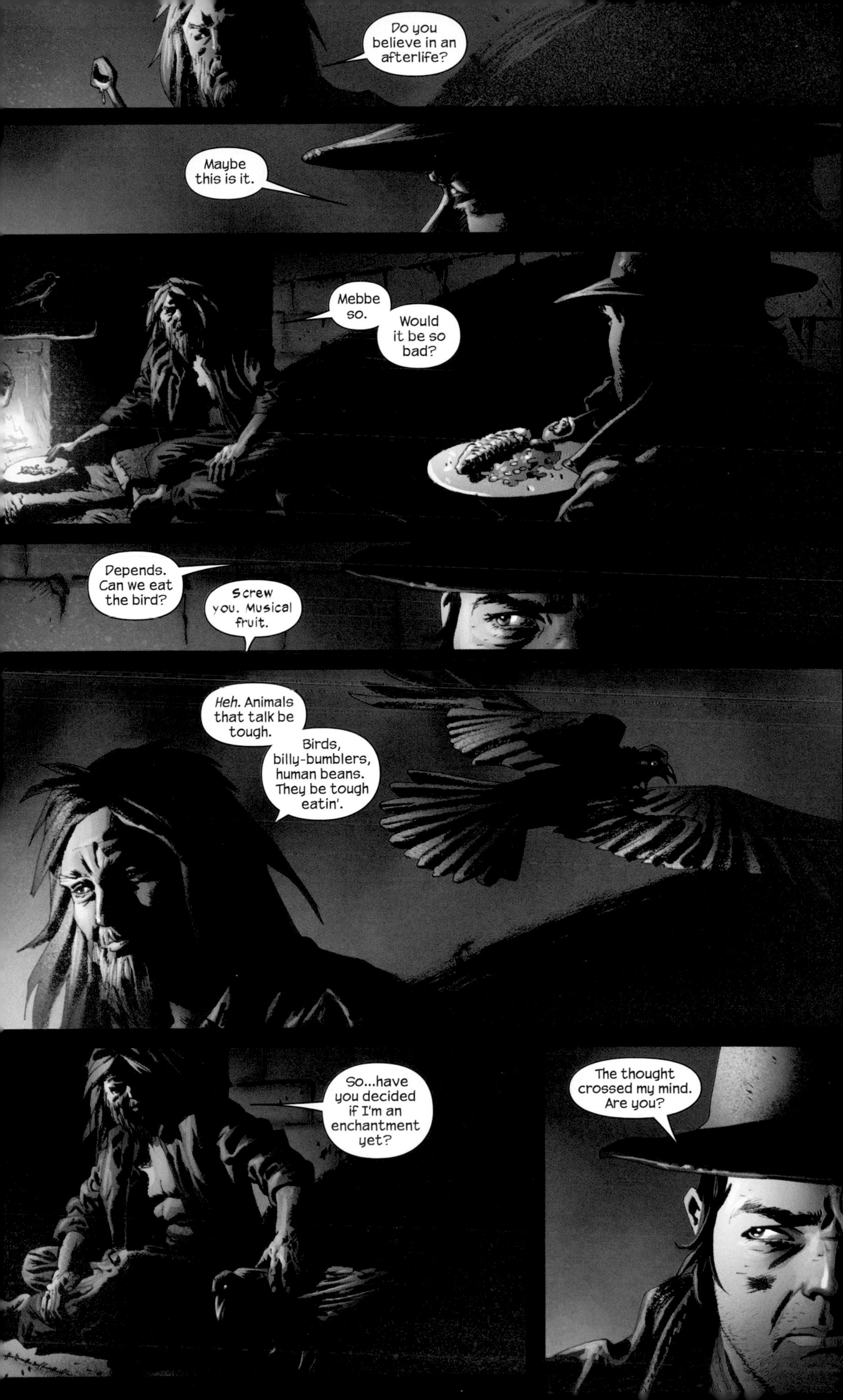
Do you believe in an afterlife?
Maybe this is it.
Mebbe so.
Would it be so bad?
Depends. Can we eat the bird?
Screw you. Musical fruit.
Heh. Animals that talk be tough.
Birds, billy-bumblers, human beans. They be tough eatin'.
So...have you decided if I'm an enchantment yet?
The thought crossed my mind. Are you?

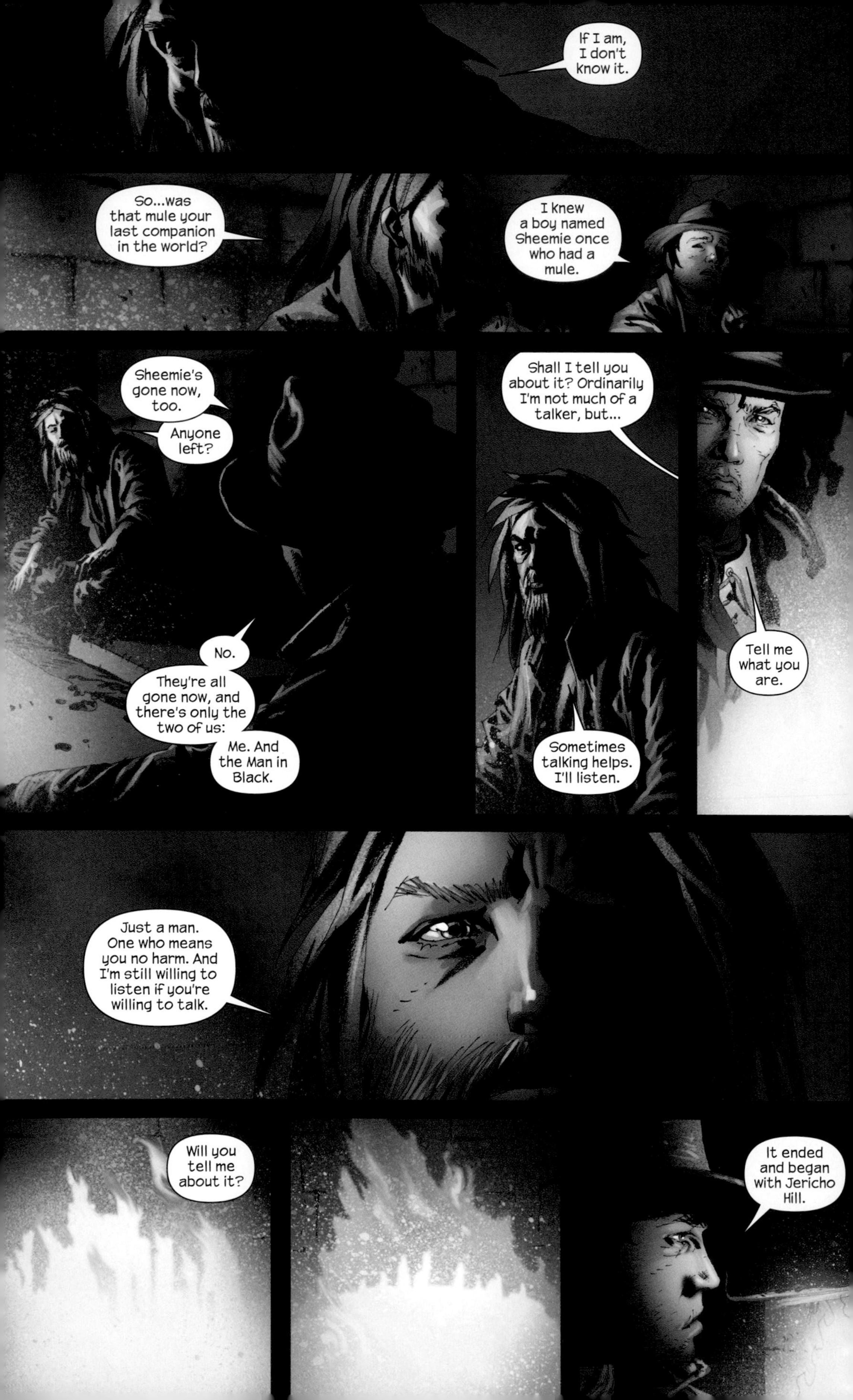
If I am, I don't know it.
So...was that mule your last companion in the world?
I knew a boy named Sheemie once who had a mule.
Sheemie's gone now, too.
Anyone left?
No.
They're all gone now, and there's only the two of us:
Me. And the Man in Black.
Shall I tell you about it? Ordinarily I'm not much of a talker, but...
Sometimes talking helps. I'll listen.
Tell me what you are.
Just a man. One who means you no harm. And I'm still willing to listen if you're willing to talk.
Will you tell me about it?
It ended and began with Jericho Hill.

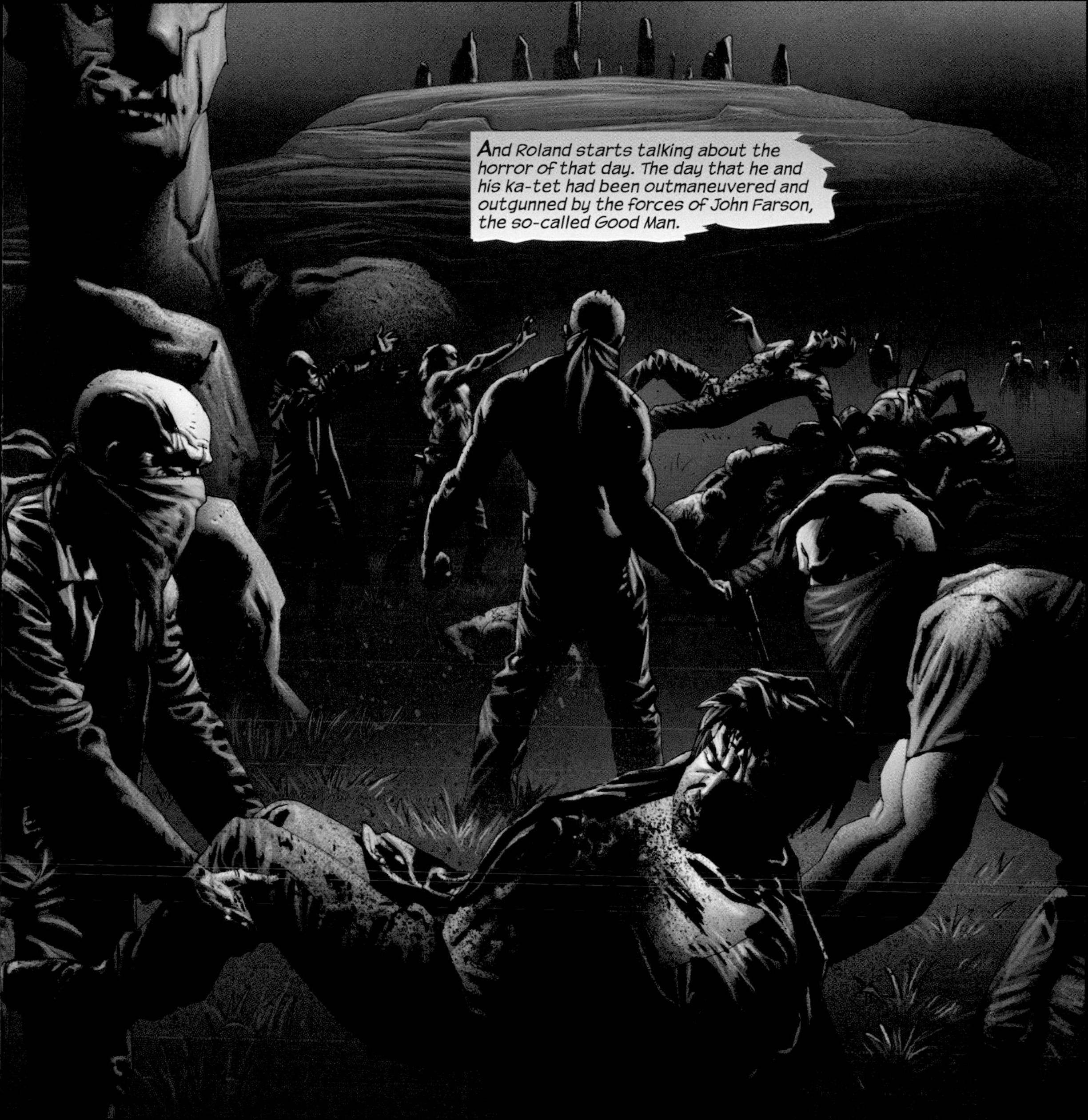
And Roland starts talking about the horror of that day. The day that he and his ka-tet had been outmaneuvered and outgunned by the forces of John Farson, the so-called Good Man.

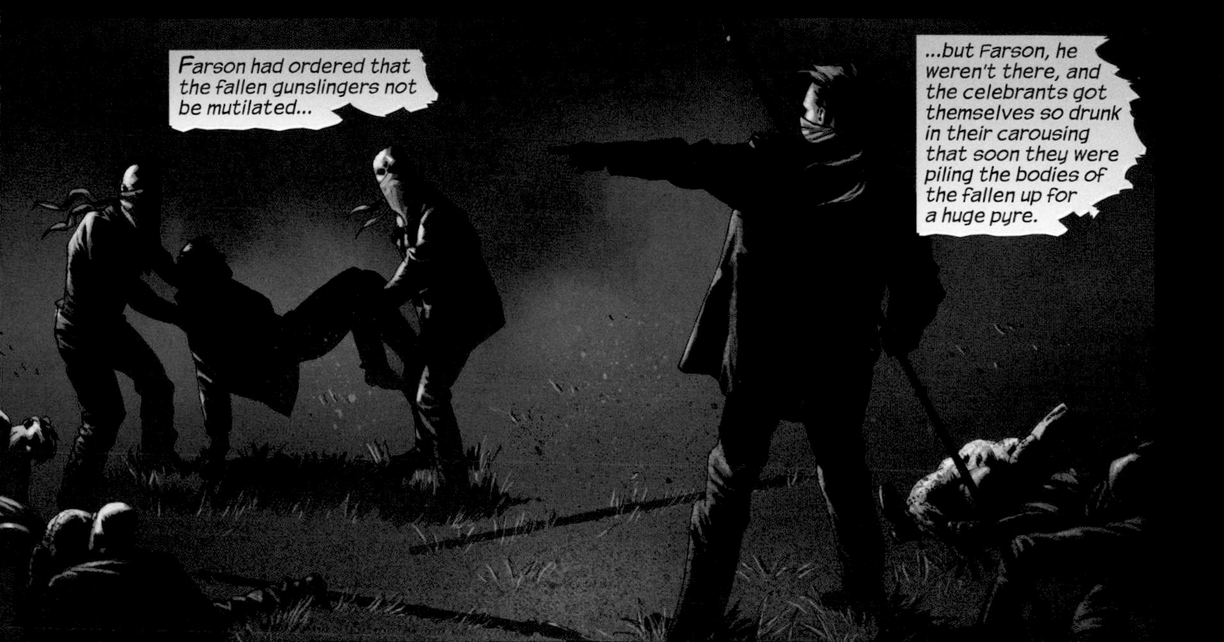
Farson had ordered that the fallen gunslingers not be mutilated...
...but Farson, he weren't there, and the celebrants got themselves so drunk in their carousing that soon they were piling the bodies of the fallen up for a huge pyre.

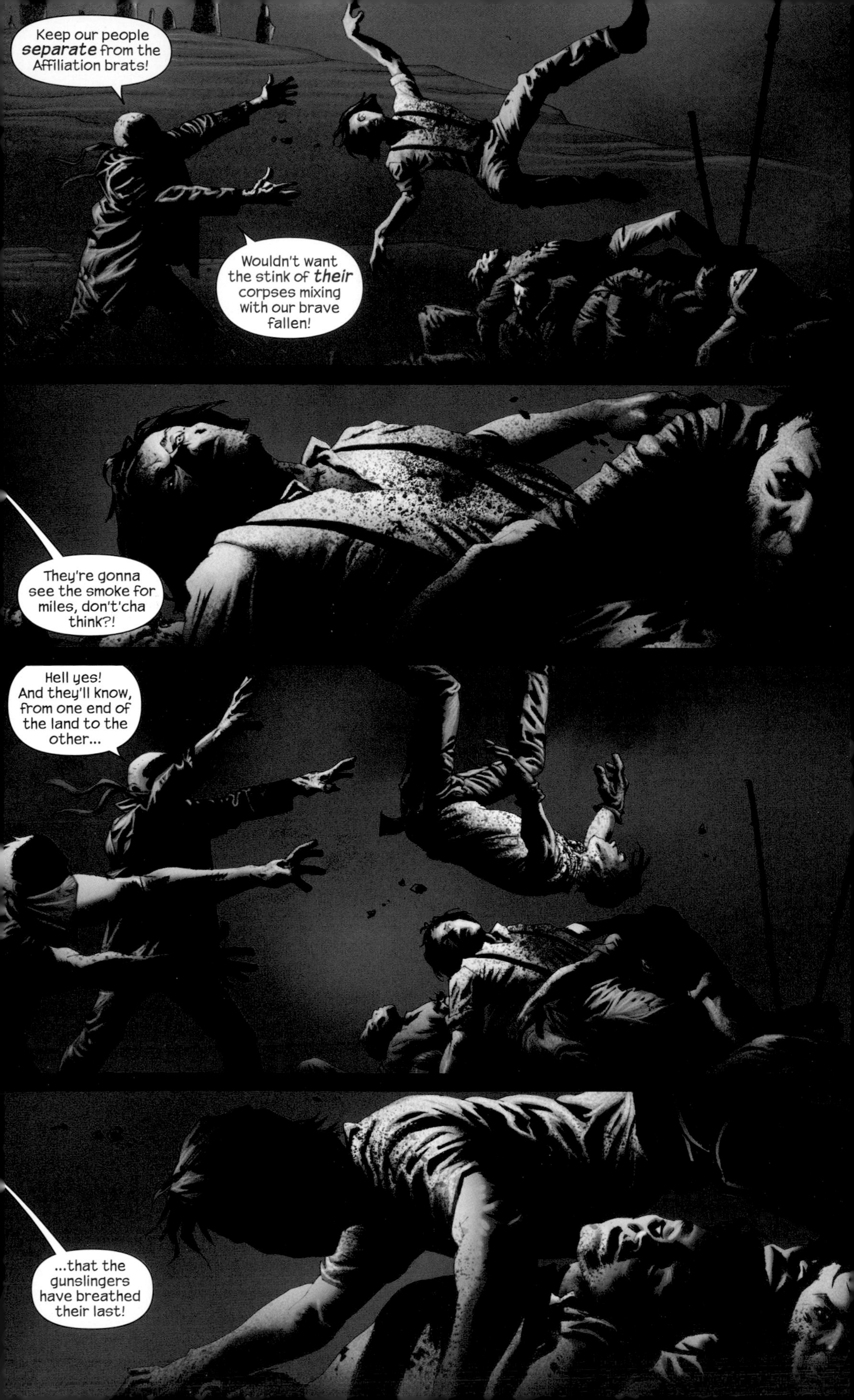
Keep our people separate from the Affiliation brats!
Wouldn't want the stink of their corpses mixing with our brave fallen!
They're gonna see the smoke for miles, don't'cha think?!
Hell yes! And they'll know, from one end of the land to the other...
...that the gunslingers have breathed their last!

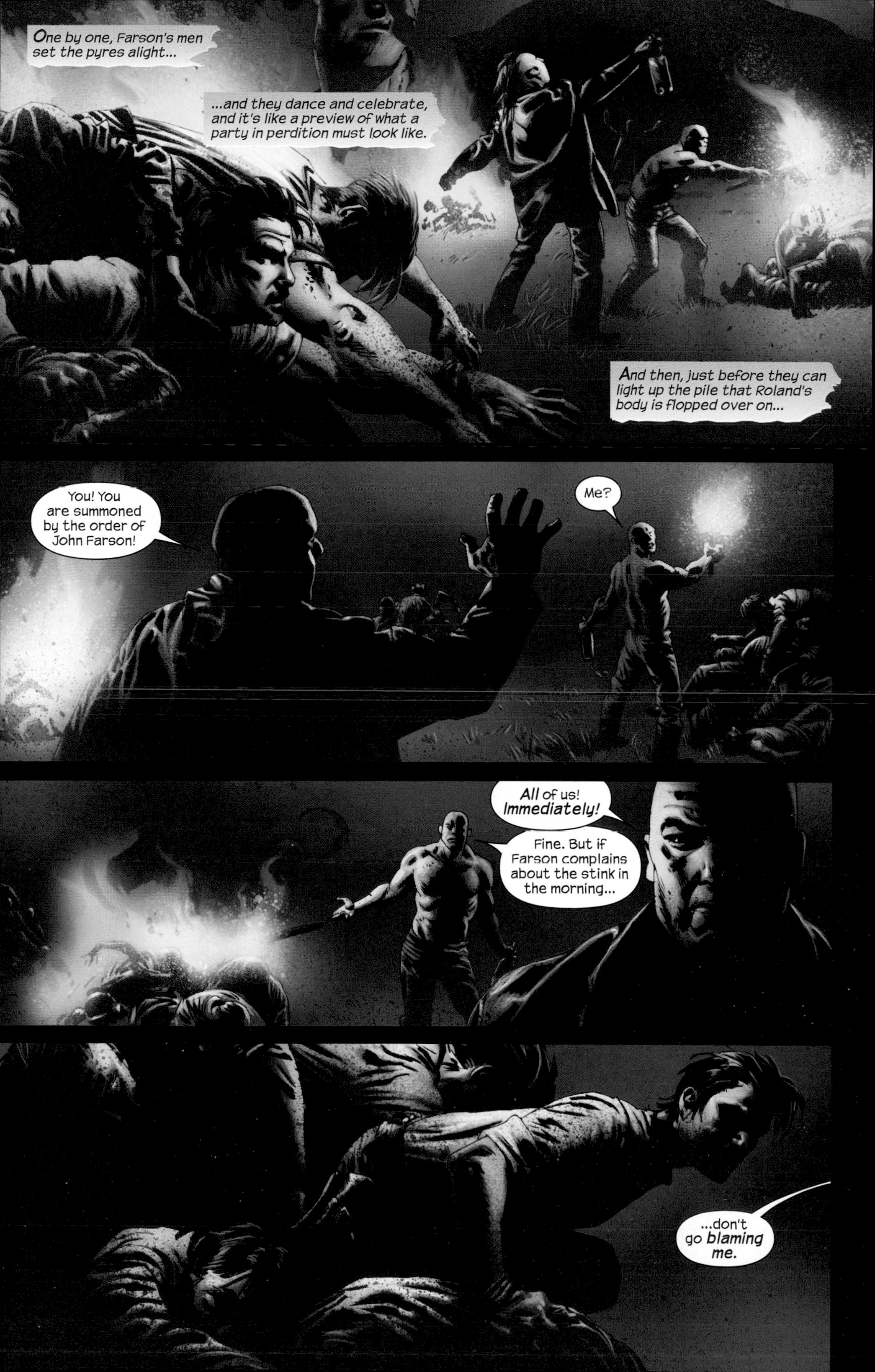
One by one, Farson's men set the pyres alight...
...and they dance and celebrate, and it's like a preview of what a party in perdition must look like.
And then, just before they can light up the pile that Roland's body is flopped over on...
You! You are summoned by the order of John Farson!
Me?
All of us! Immediately!
Fine. But if Farson complains about the stink in the morning...
...don't go blaming me.

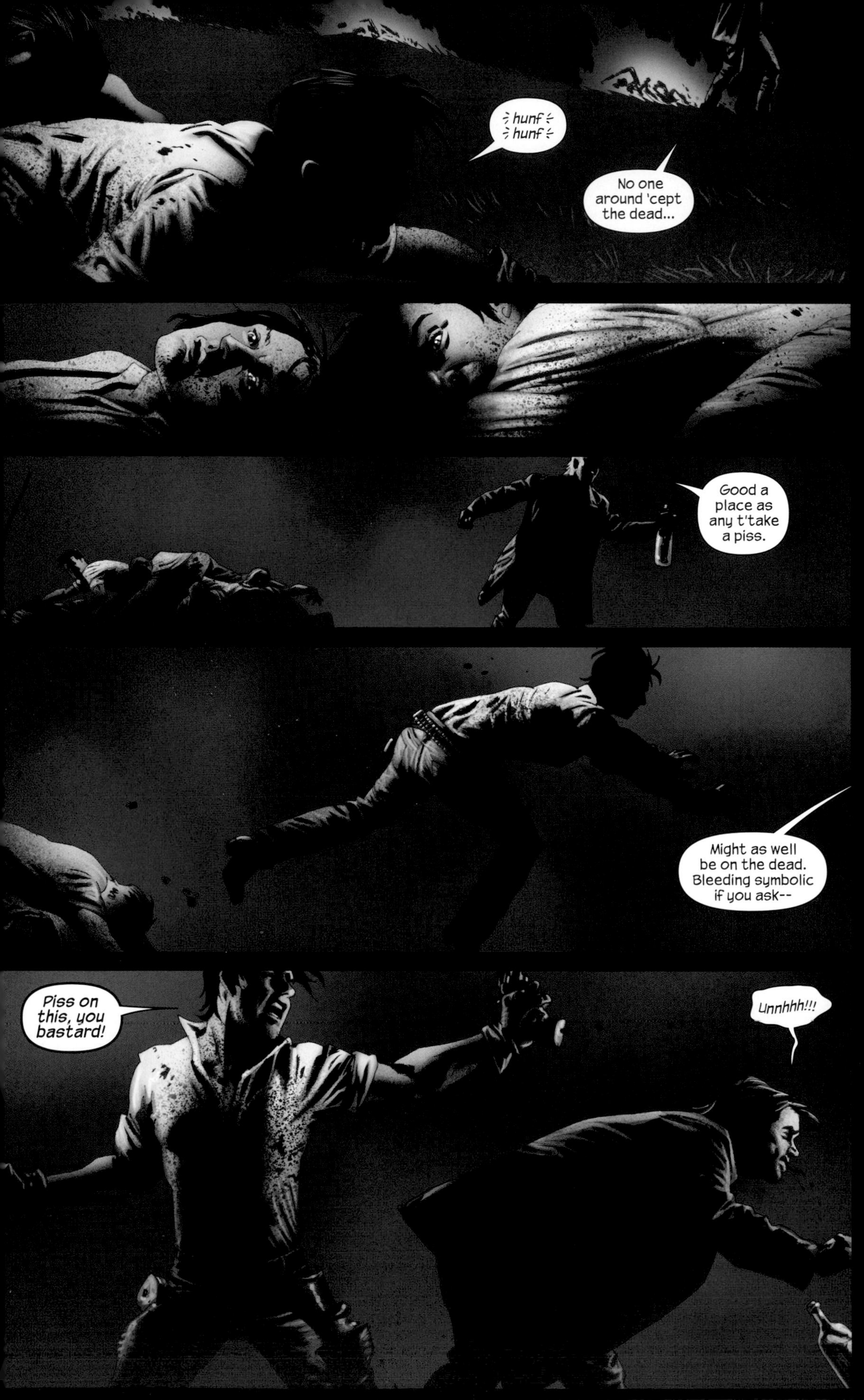
hunf
hunf
No one around 'cept the dead...
Good a place as any t'take a piss.
Might as well be on the dead. Bleeding symbolic if you ask--
Piss on this, you bastard!
Unnhhh!!!

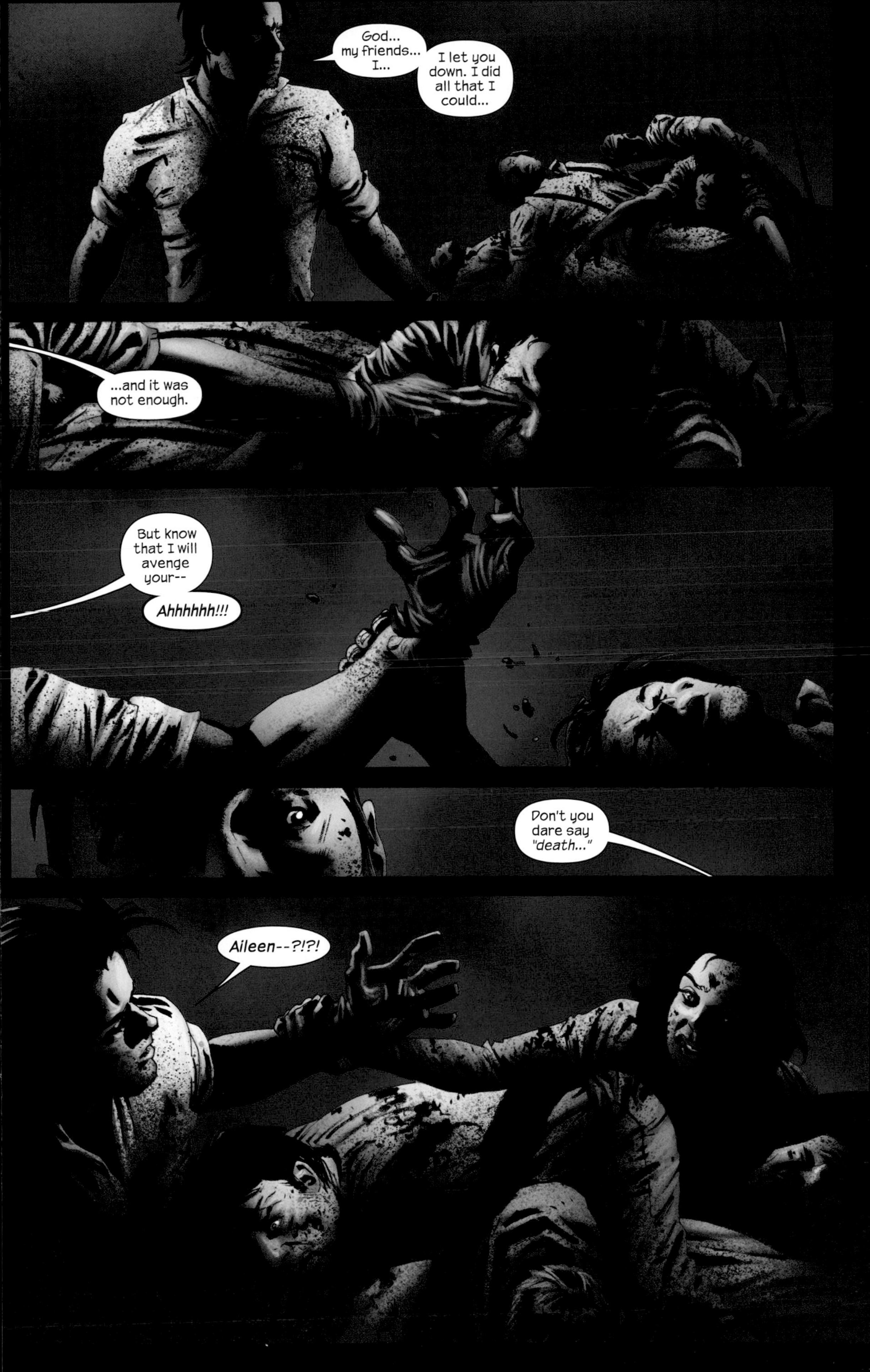
God... my friends... I...
I let you down. I did all that I could...
...and it was not enough.
But know that I will avenge your--
Ahhhhhh!!!
Don't you dare say "death..."
Aileen--?!?!

STEPHEN KING

THE DARK TOWER
~ THE GUNSLINGER ~

THE JOURNEY BEGINS
CHAPTER TWO

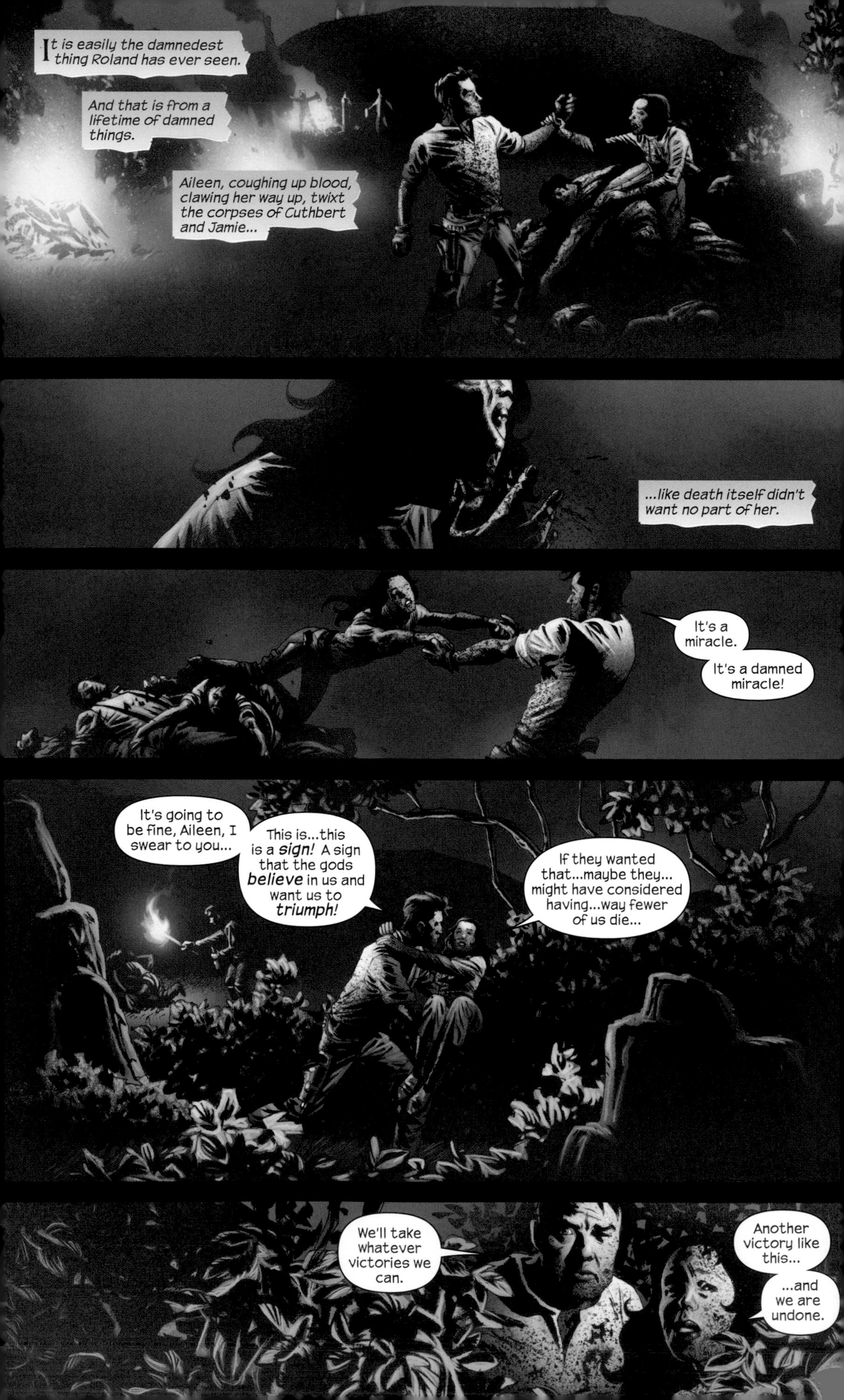
It is easily the damnedest thing Roland has ever seen.
And that is from a lifetime of damned things.
Aileen, coughing up blood, clawing her way up, twixt the corpses of Cuthbert and Jamie...
...like death itself didn't want no part of her.
It's a miracle.
It's a damned miracle!
It's going to be fine, Aileen, I swear to you...
This is...this is a *sign!* A sign that the gods ***believe*** in us and want us to ***triumph!***
If they wanted that...maybe they... might have considered having...way fewer of us die...
We'll take whatever victories we can.
Another victory like this...
...and we are undone.

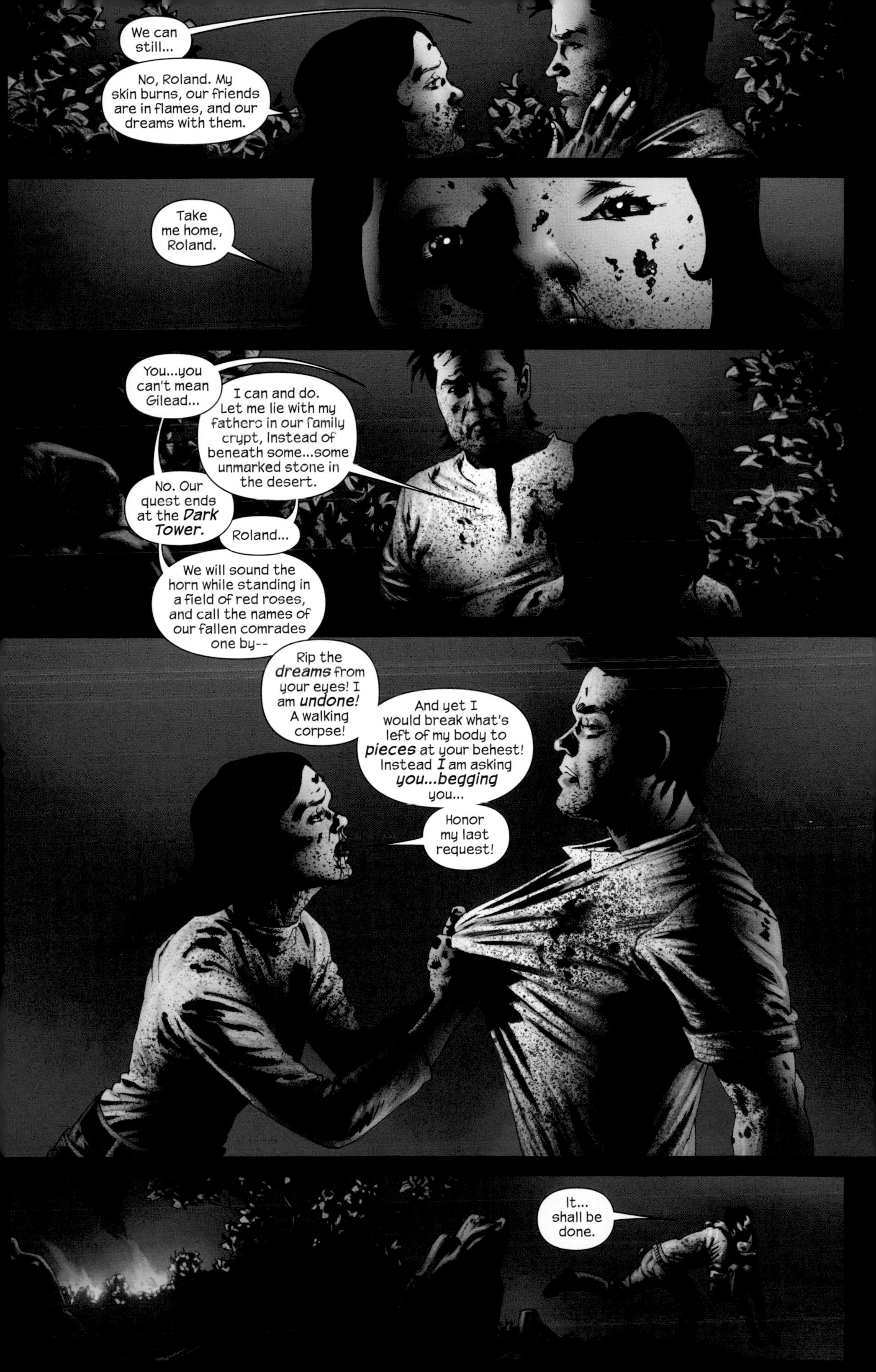
We can still...
No, Roland. My skin burns, our friends are in flames, and our dreams with them.
Take me home, Roland.
You...you can't mean Gilead...
I can and do. Let me lie with my fathers in our family crypt, instead of beneath some...some unmarked stone in the desert.
No. Our quest ends at the *Dark Tower.*
Roland...
We will sound the horn while standing in a field of red roses, and call the names of our fallen comrades one by--
Rip the *dreams* from your eyes! I am *undone!* A walking corpse!
And yet I would break what's left of my body to *pieces* at your behest! Instead *I* am asking *you...begging* you...
Honor my last request!
It... shall be done.

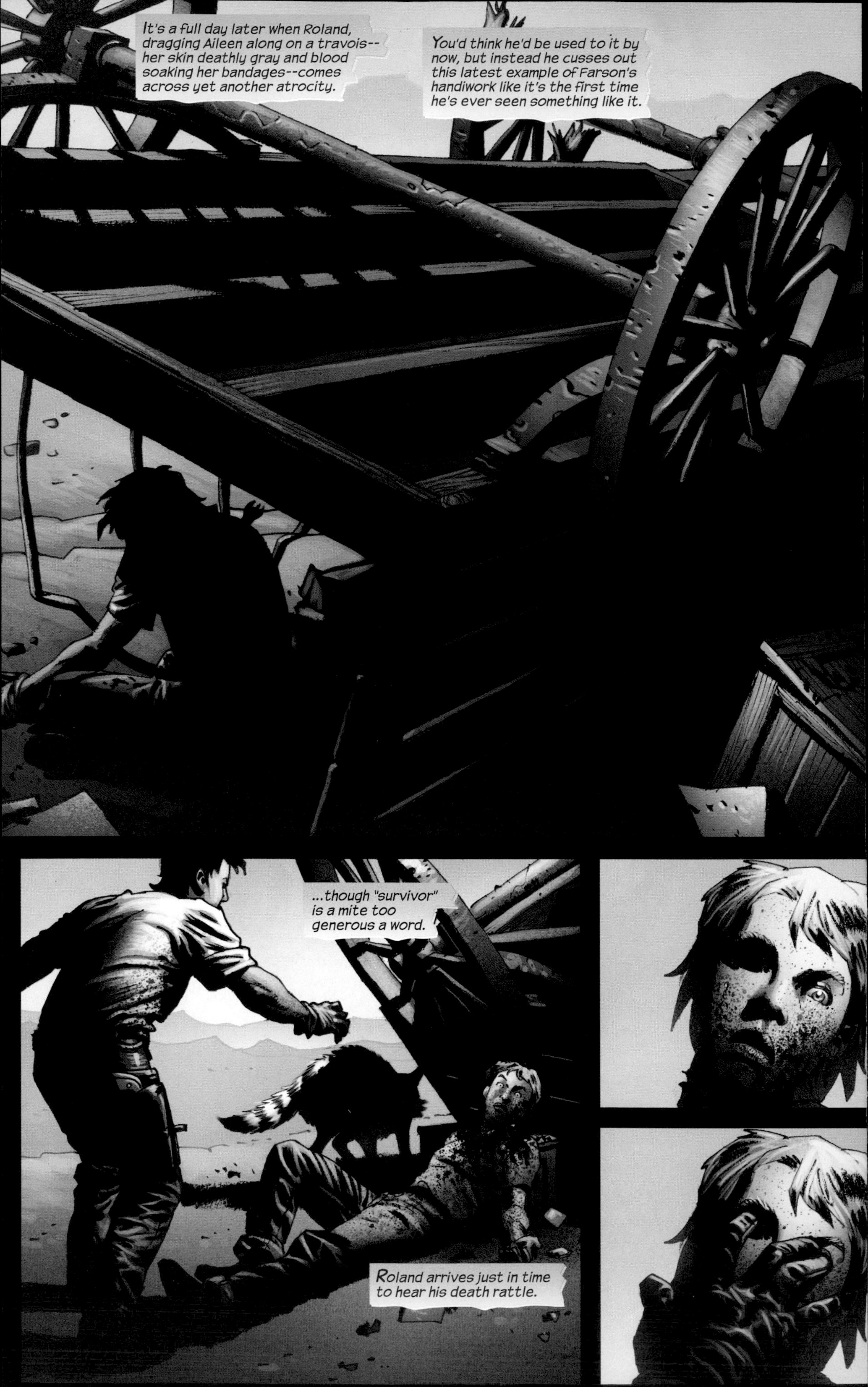
It's a full day later when Roland, dragging Aileen along on a travois--her skin deathly gray and blood soaking her bandages--comes across yet another atrocity.
You'd think he'd be used to it by now, but instead he cusses out this latest example of Farson's handiwork like it's the first time he's ever seen something like it.
...though "survivor" is a mite too generous a word.
Roland arrives just in time to hear his death rattle.

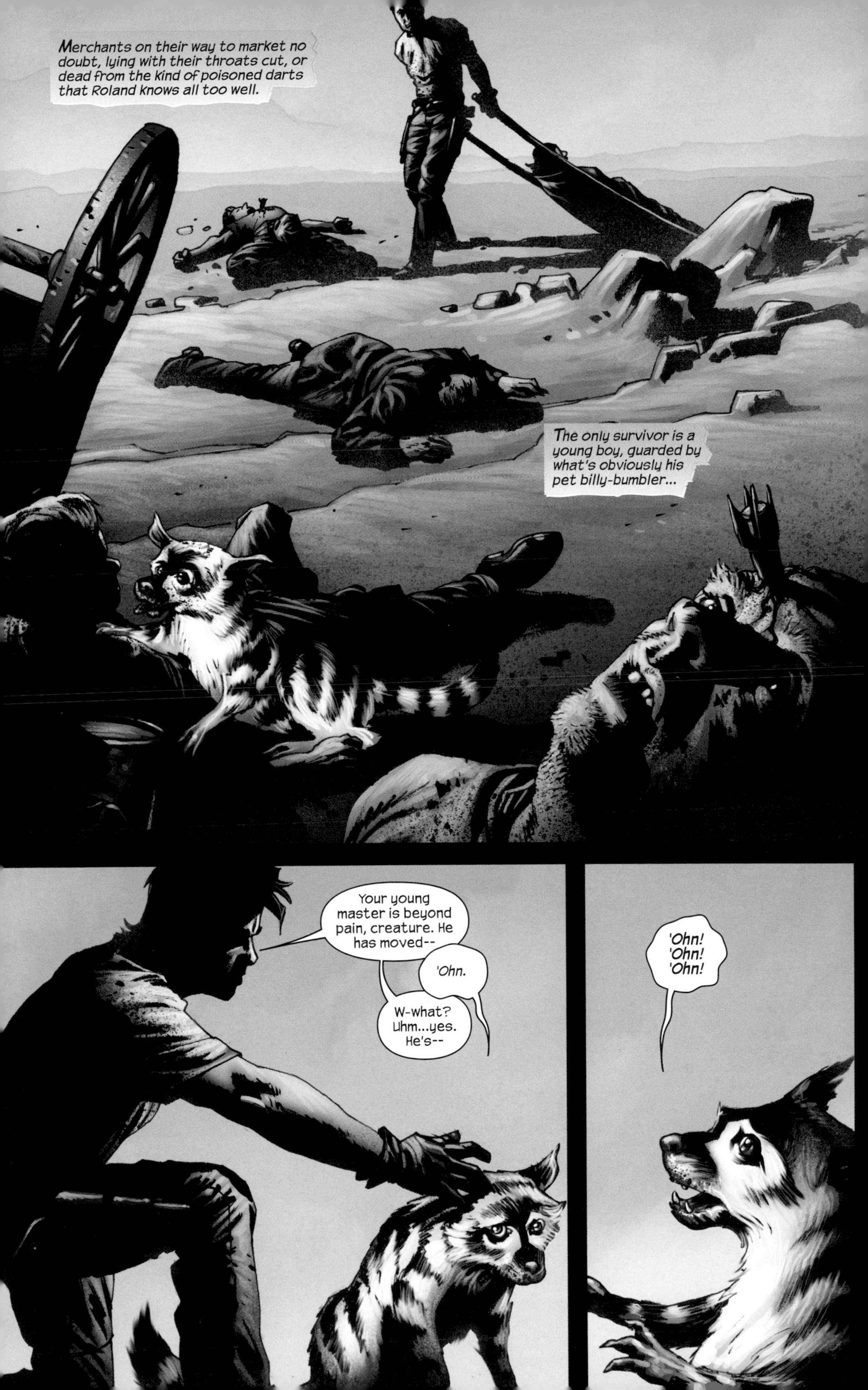
Merchants on their way to market no doubt, lying with their throats cut, or dead from the kind of poisoned darts that Roland knows all too well.
The only survivor is a young boy, guarded by what's obviously his pet billy-bumbler...
Your young master is beyond pain, creature. He has moved--
'Ohn.
W-what? Uhm...yes. He's--
'Ohn! 'Ohn! 'Ohn!

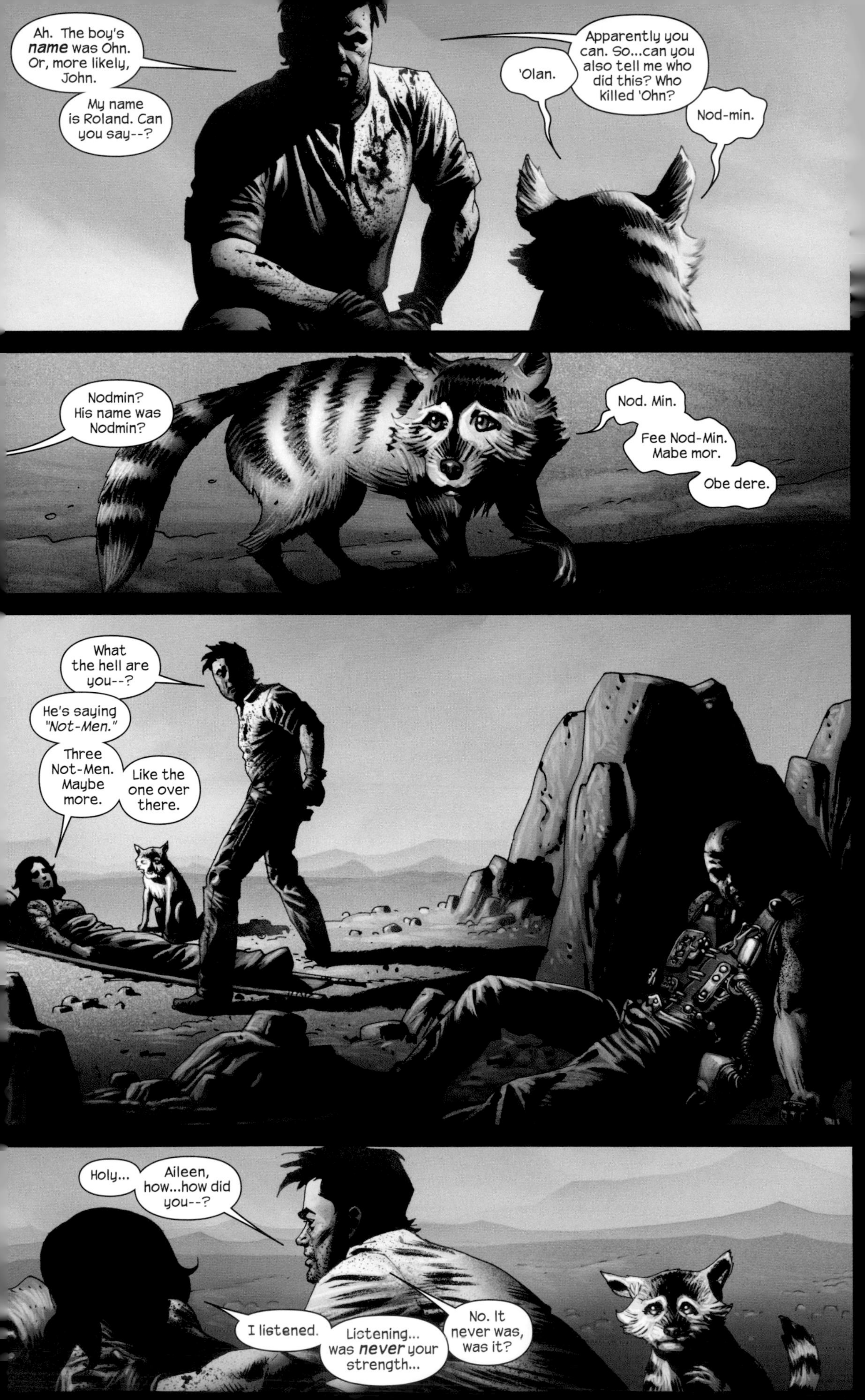
Ah. The boy's name was Ohn. Or, more likely, John.
My name is Roland. Can you say--?
'Olan.
Apparently you can. So...can you also tell me who did this? Who killed 'Ohn?
Nod-min.
Nodmin? His name was Nodmin?
Nod. Min.
Fee Nod-Min. Mabe mor.
Obe dere.
What the hell are you--?
He's saying "Not-Men."
Three Not-Men. Maybe more.
Like the one over there.
Holy...
Aileen, how...how did you--?
I listened.
Listening... was never your strength...
No. It never was, was it?

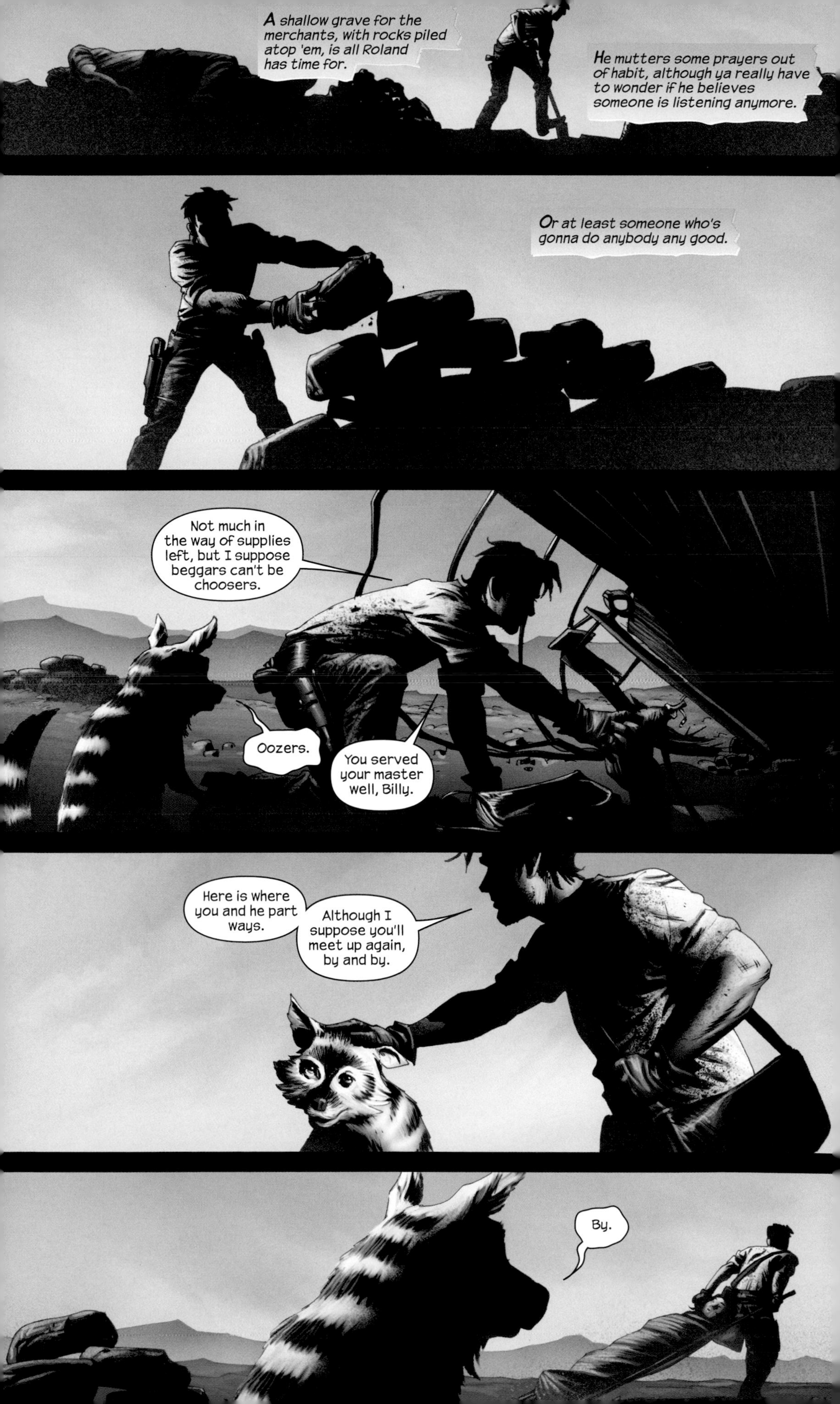
A shallow grave for the merchants, with rocks piled atop 'em, is all Roland has time for.
He mutters some prayers out of habit, although ya really have to wonder if he believes someone is listening anymore.
Or at least someone who's gonna do anybody any good.
Not much in the way of supplies left, but I suppose beggars can't be choosers.
Oozers.
You served your master well, Billy.
Here is where you and he part ways.
Although I suppose you'll meet up again, by and by.
By.

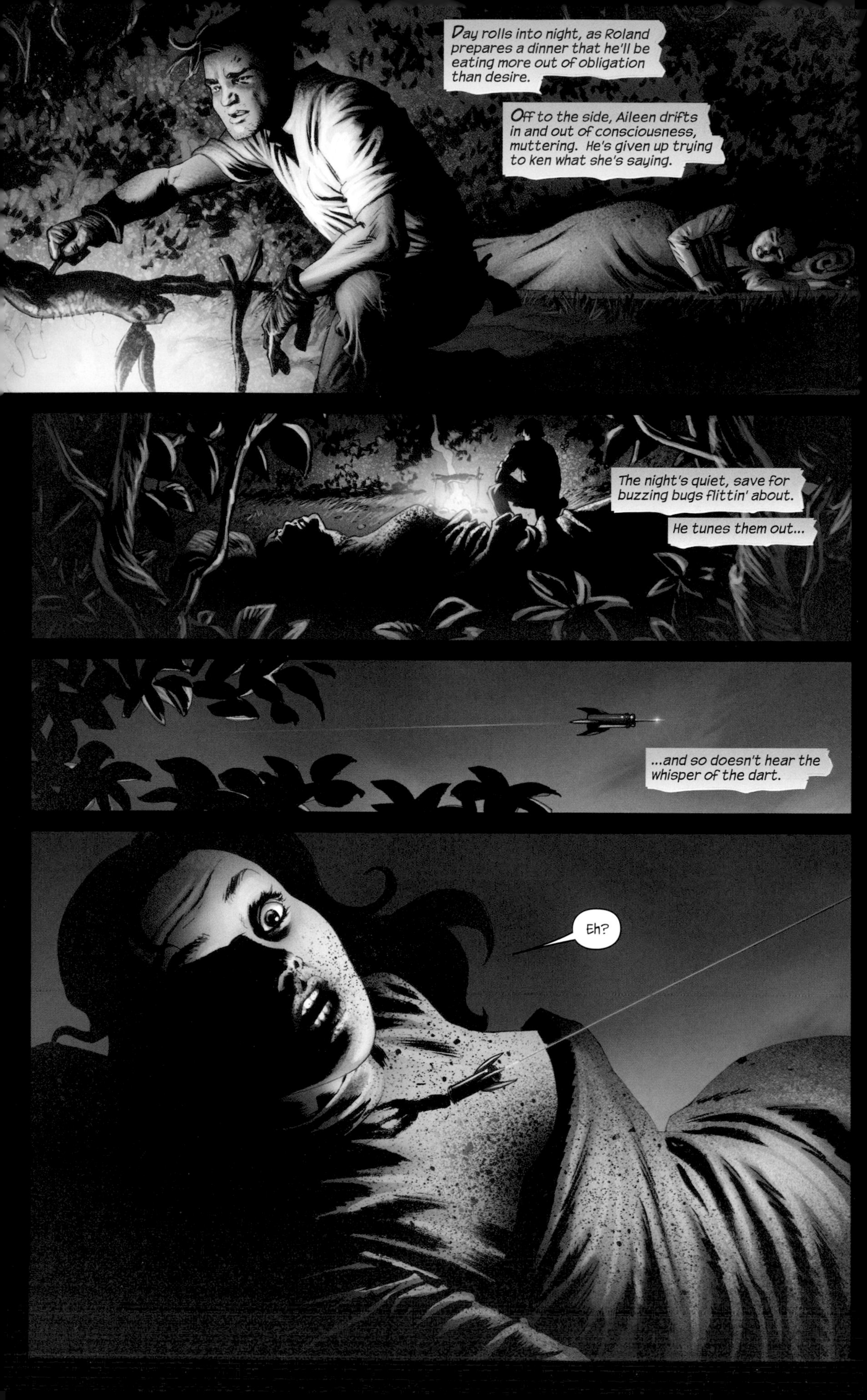
Day rolls into night, as Roland prepares a dinner that he'll be eating more out of obligation than desire.
Off to the side, Aileen drifts in and out of consciousness, muttering. He's given up trying to ken what she's saying.
The night's quiet, save for buzzing bugs flittin' about.
He tunes them out...
...and so doesn't hear the whisper of the dart.
Eh?

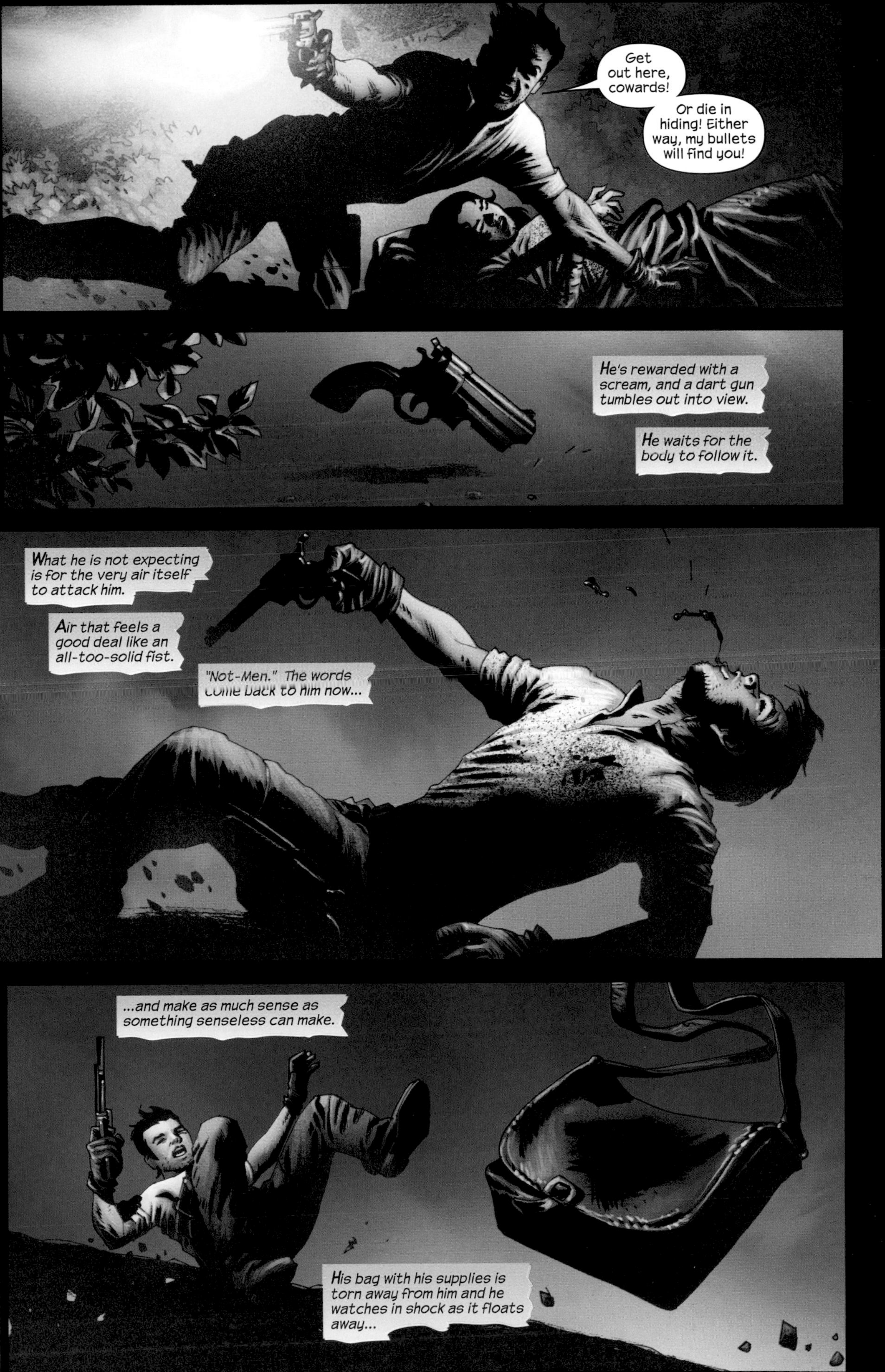
Get out here, cowards!
Or die in hiding! Either way, my bullets will find you!
He's rewarded with a scream, and a dart gun tumbles out into view.
He waits for the body to follow it.
What he is not expecting is for the very air itself to attack him.
Air that feels a good deal like an all-too-solid fist.
"Not-Men." The words come back to him now...
...and make as much sense as something senseless can make.
His bag with his supplies is torn away from him and he watches in shock as it floats away...

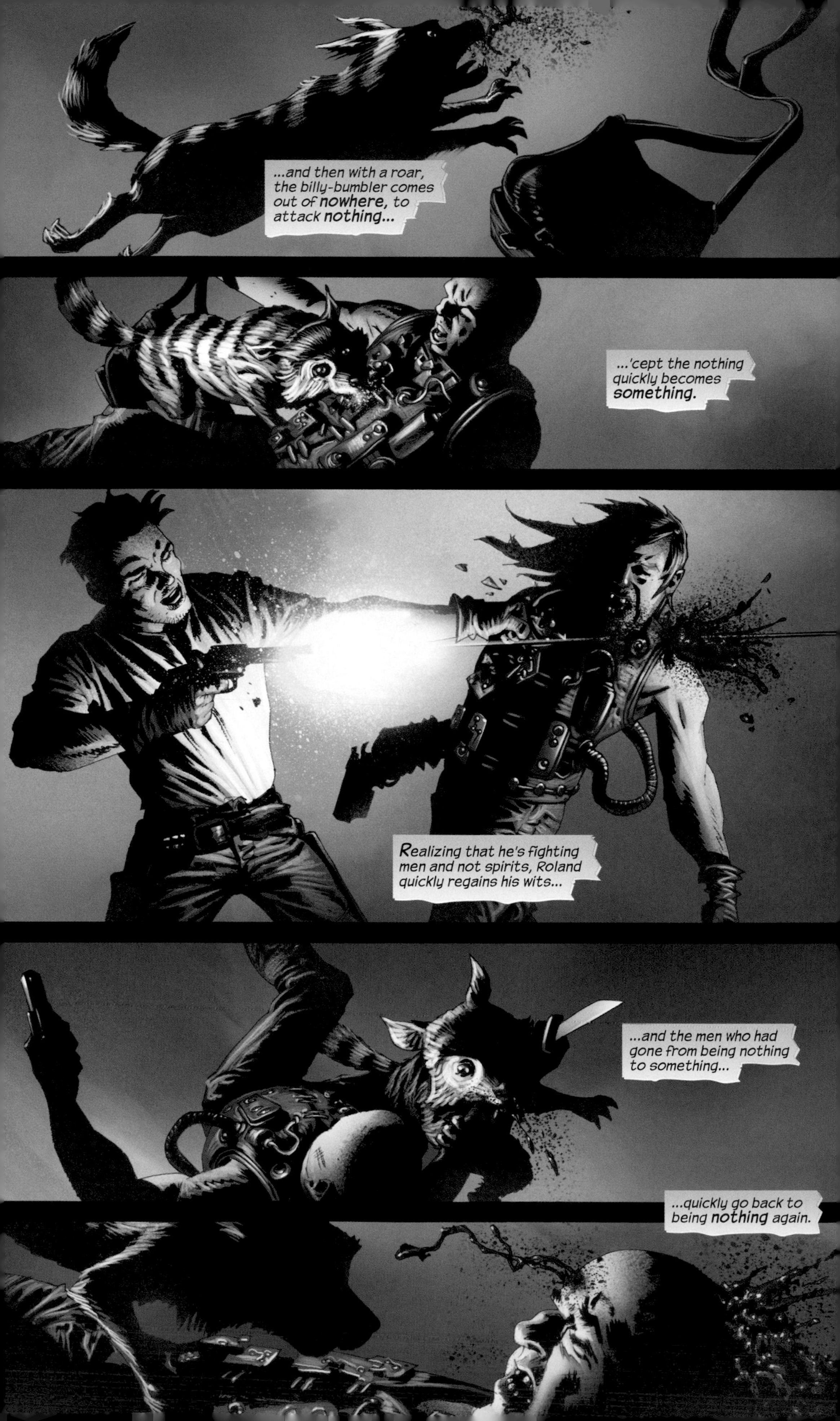
...and then with a roar, the billy-bumbler comes out of nowhere, to attack nothing...
...'cept the nothing quickly becomes something.
Realizing that he's fighting men and not spirits, Roland quickly regains his wits...
...and the men who had gone from being nothing to something...
...quickly go back to being nothing again.

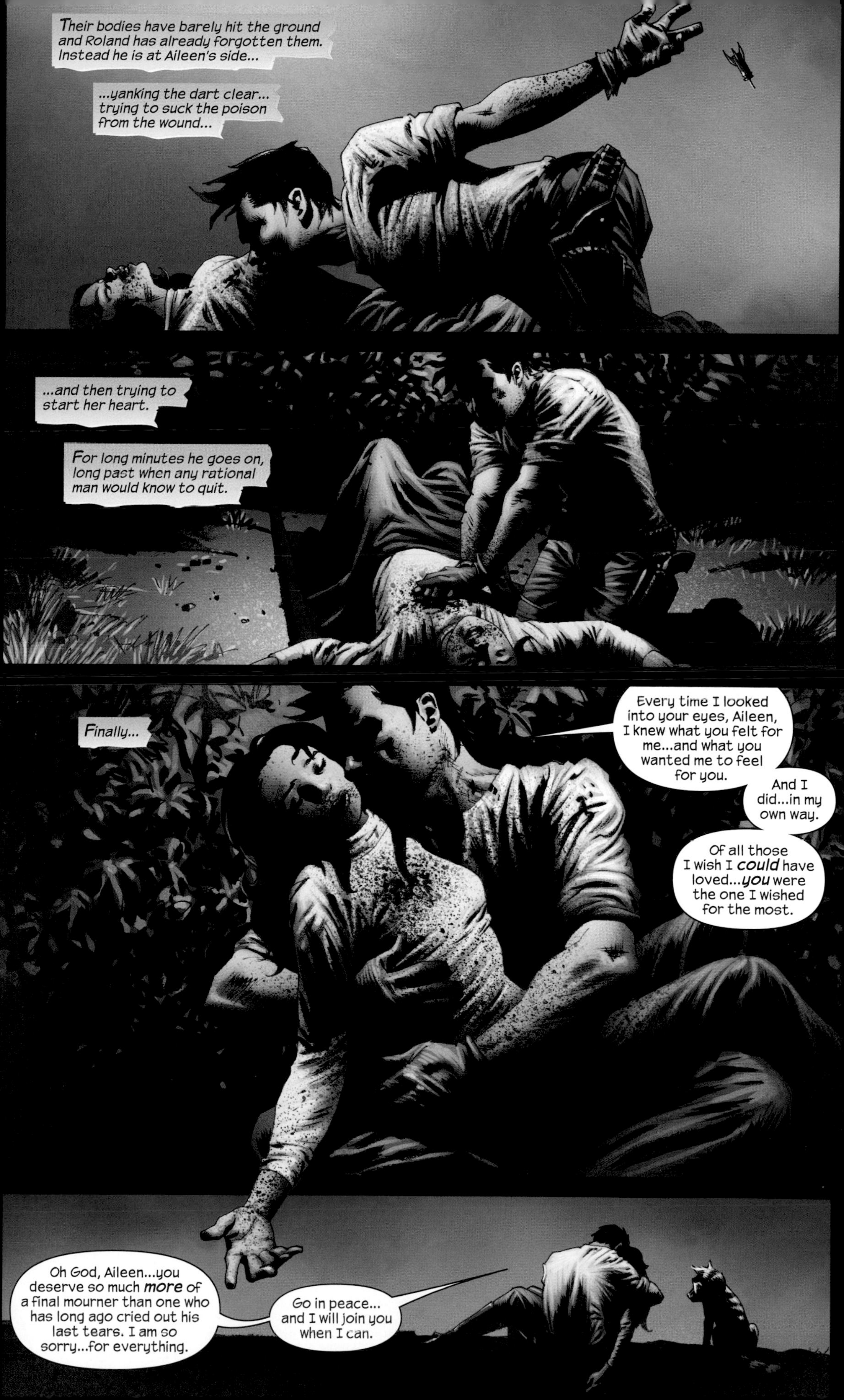
Their bodies have barely hit the ground and Roland has already forgotten them. Instead he is at Aileen's side...
...yanking the dart clear... trying to suck the poison from the wound...
...and then trying to start her heart.
For long minutes he goes on, long past when any rational man would know to quit.
Finally...
Every time I looked into your eyes, Aileen, I knew what you felt for me...and what you wanted me to feel for you.
And I did...in my own way.
Of all those I wish I could have loved...you were the one I wished for the most.
Oh God, Aileen...you deserve so much more of a final mourner than one who has long ago cried out his last tears. I am so sorry...for everything.
Go in peace... and I will join you when I can.

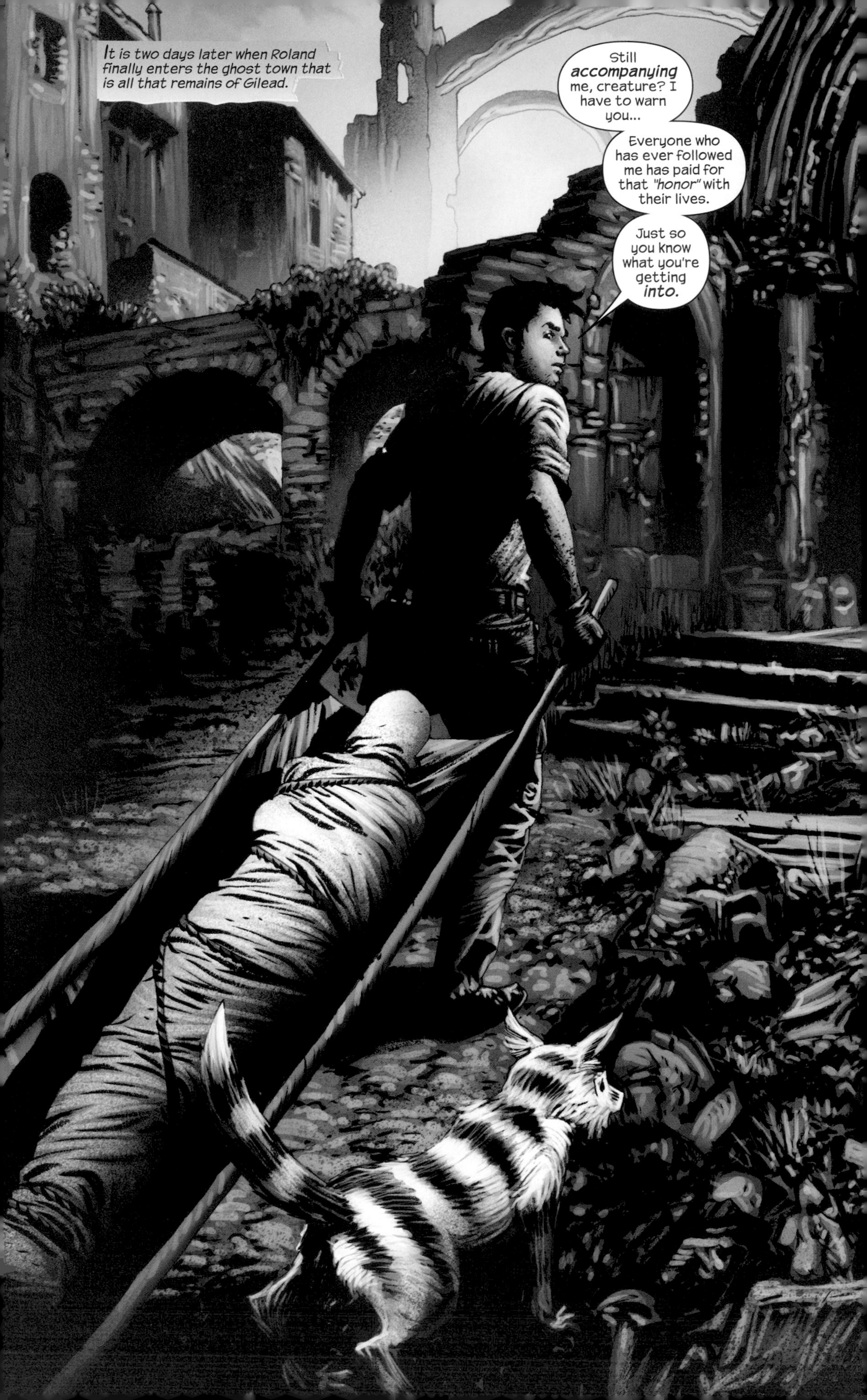
It is two days later when Roland finally enters the ghost town that is all that remains of Gilead.
Still accompanying me, creature? I have to warn you...
Everyone who has ever followed me has paid for that "honor" with their lives.
Just so you know what you're getting into.

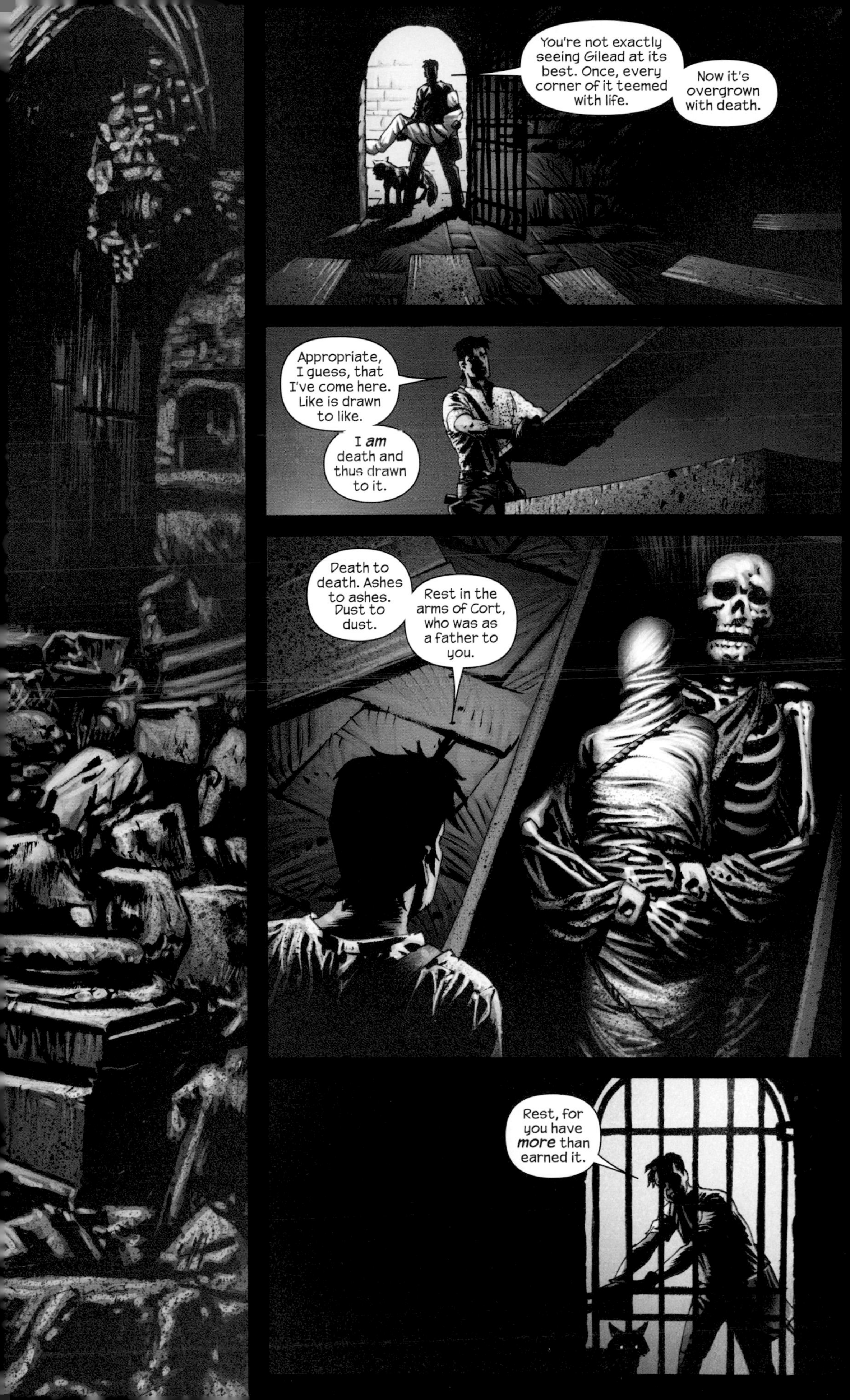
You're not exactly seeing Gilead at its best. Once, every corner of it teemed with life.
Now it's overgrown with death.
Appropriate, I guess, that I've come here. Like is drawn to like.
I *am* death and thus drawn to it.
Death to death. Ashes to ashes. Dust to dust.
Rest in the arms of Cort, who was as a father to you.
Rest, for you have *more* than earned it.

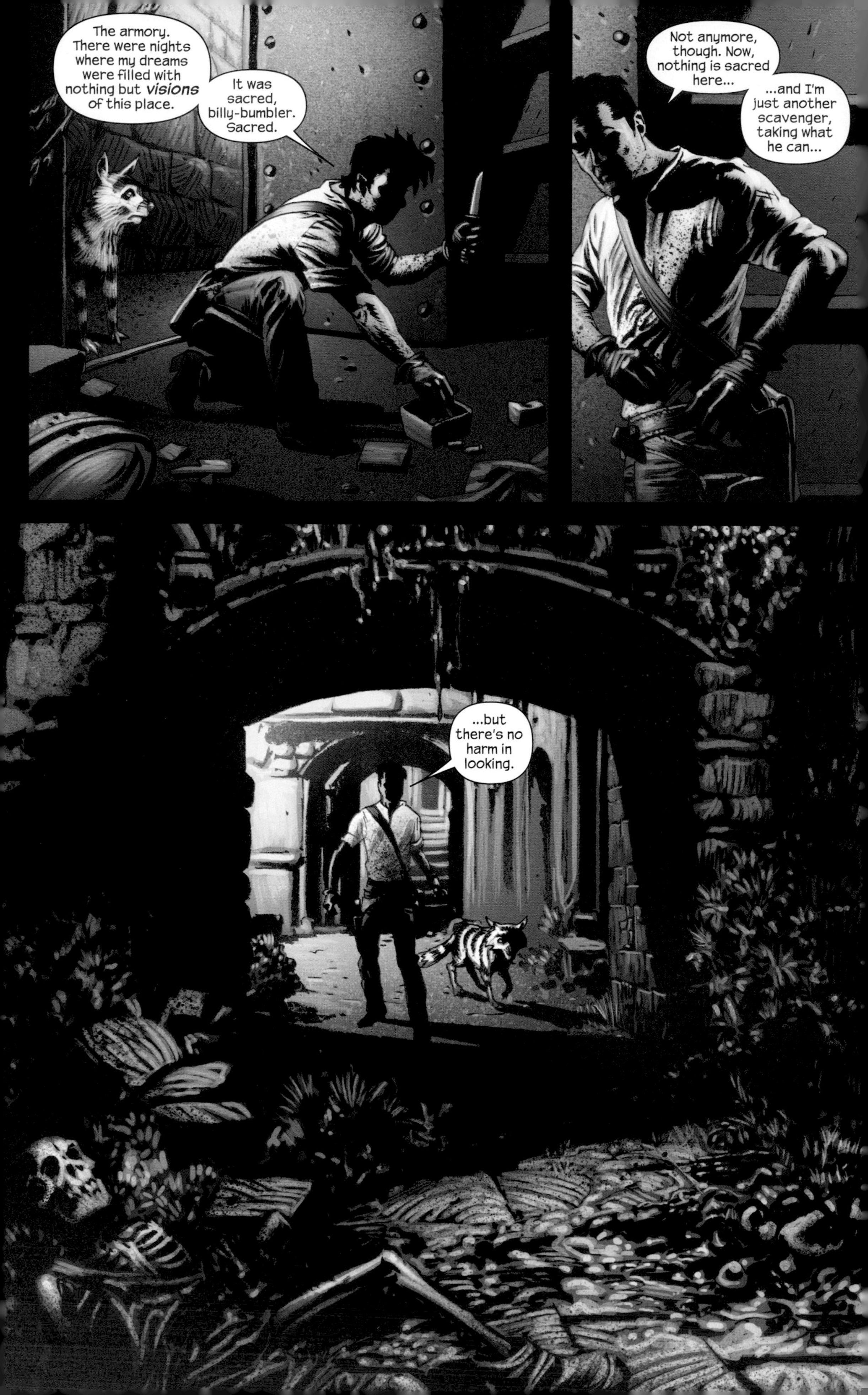

The armory. There were nights where my dreams were filled with nothing but *visions* of this place.
It was sacred, billy-bumbler. Sacred.
Not anymore, though. Now, nothing is sacred here...
...and I'm just another scavenger, taking what he can...
...but there's no harm in looking.

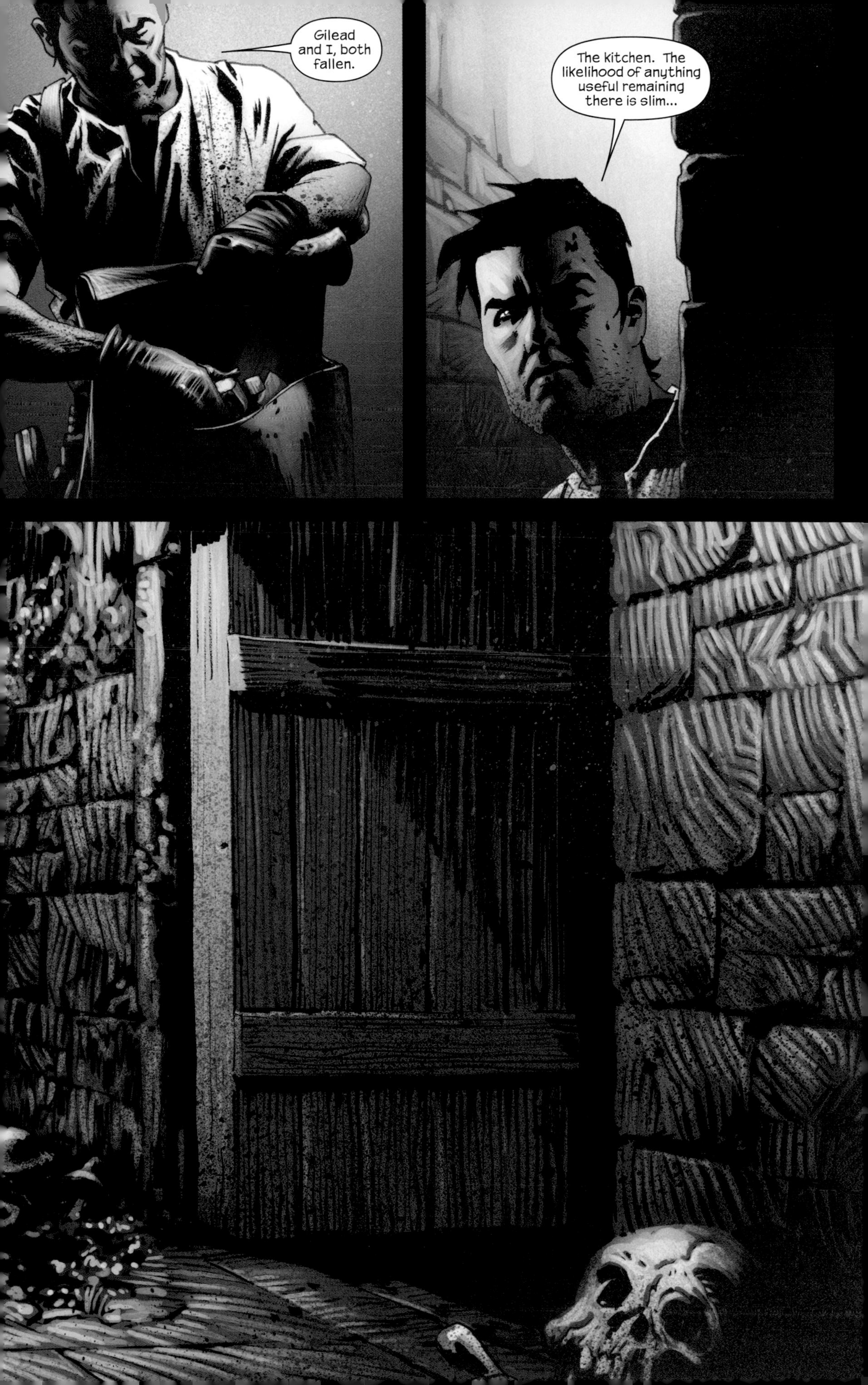
Gilead and I, both fallen.
The kitchen. The likelihood of anything useful remaining there is slim...

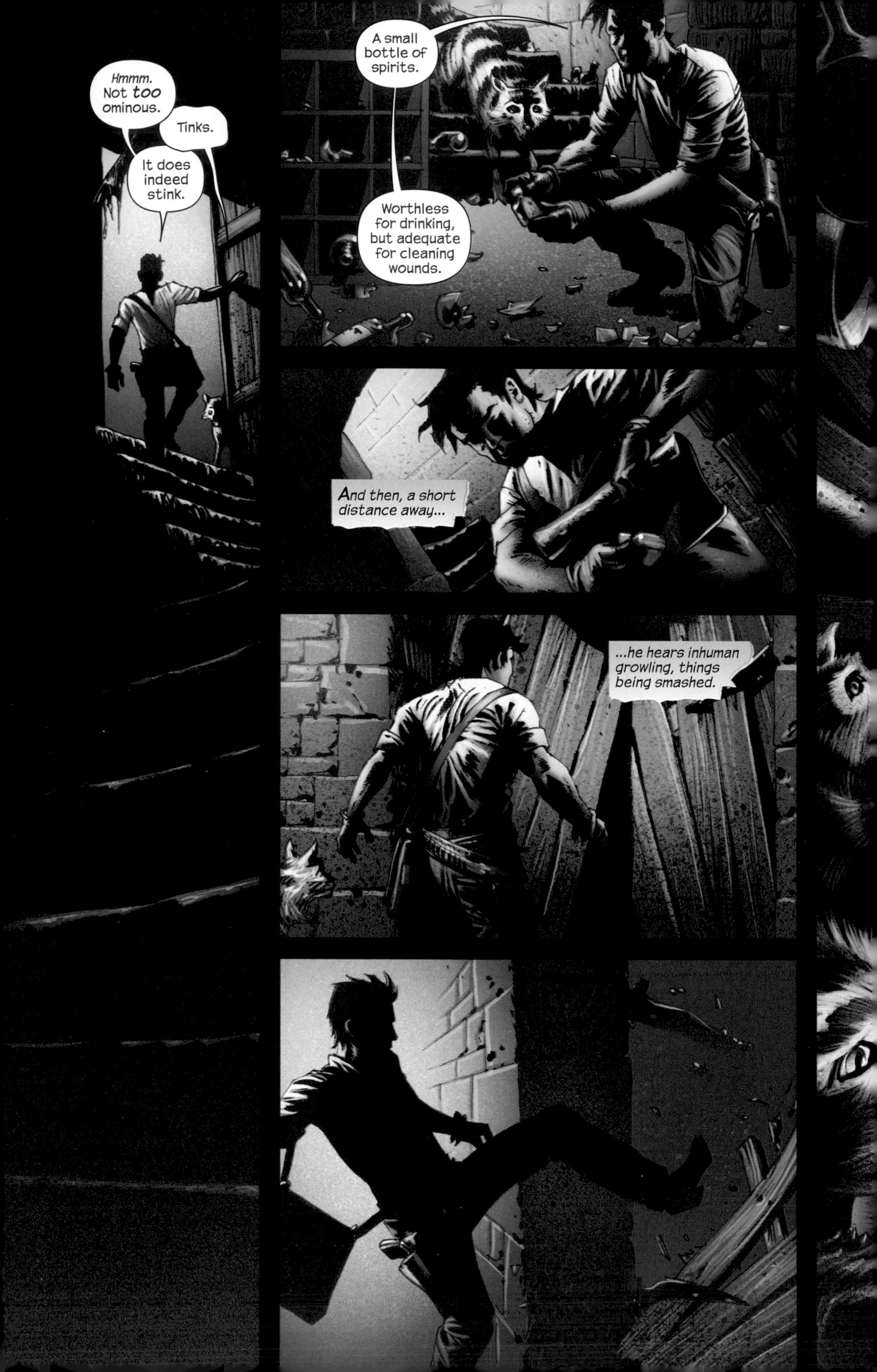
Hmmm. Not ***too*** ominous.
Tinks.
It does indeed stink.
A small bottle of spirits.
Worthless for drinking, but adequate for cleaning wounds.
And then, a short distance away...
...he hears inhuman growling, things being smashed.

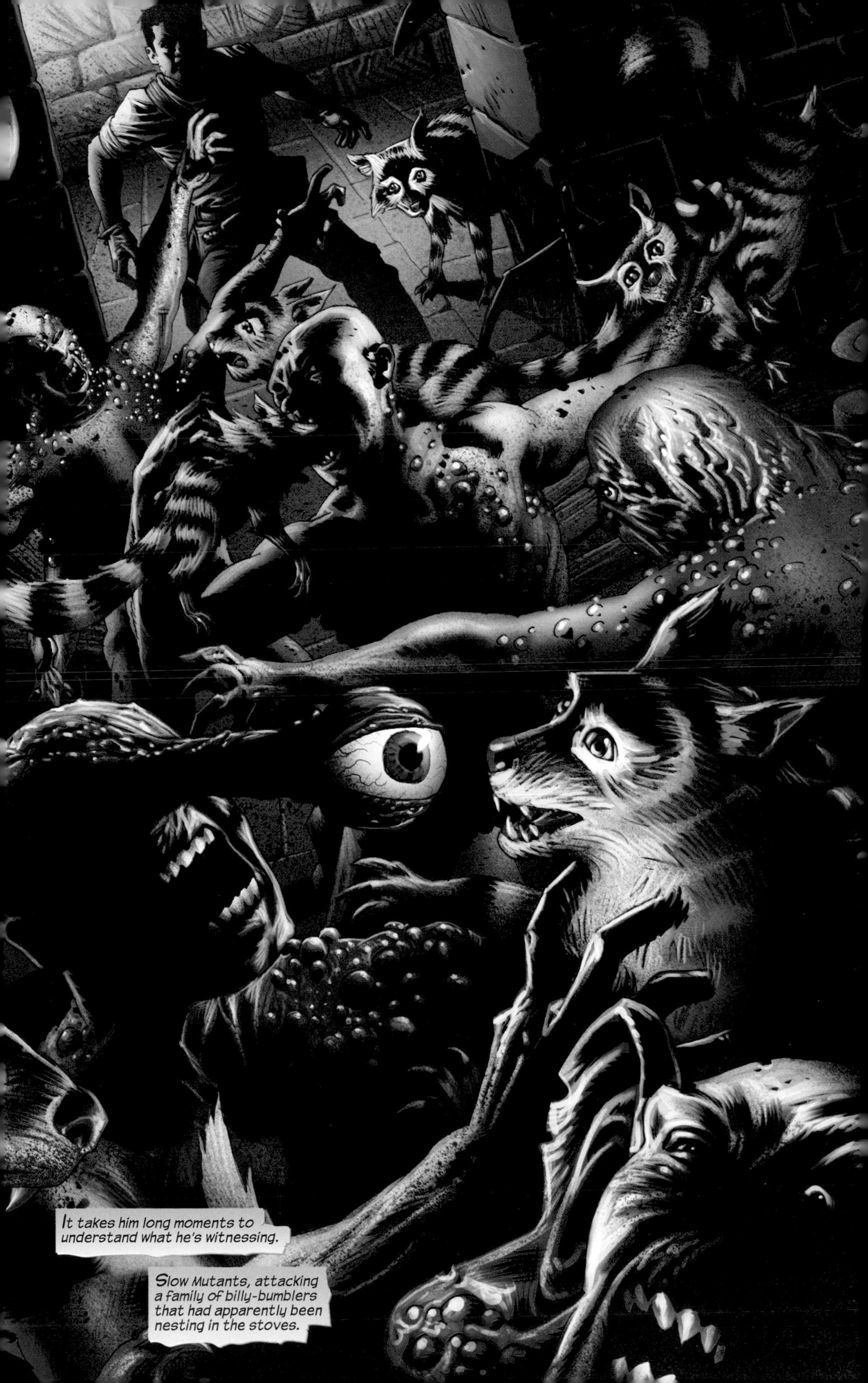
It takes him long moments to understand what he's witnessing.
Slow Mutants, attacking a family of billy-bumblers that had apparently been nesting in the stoves.

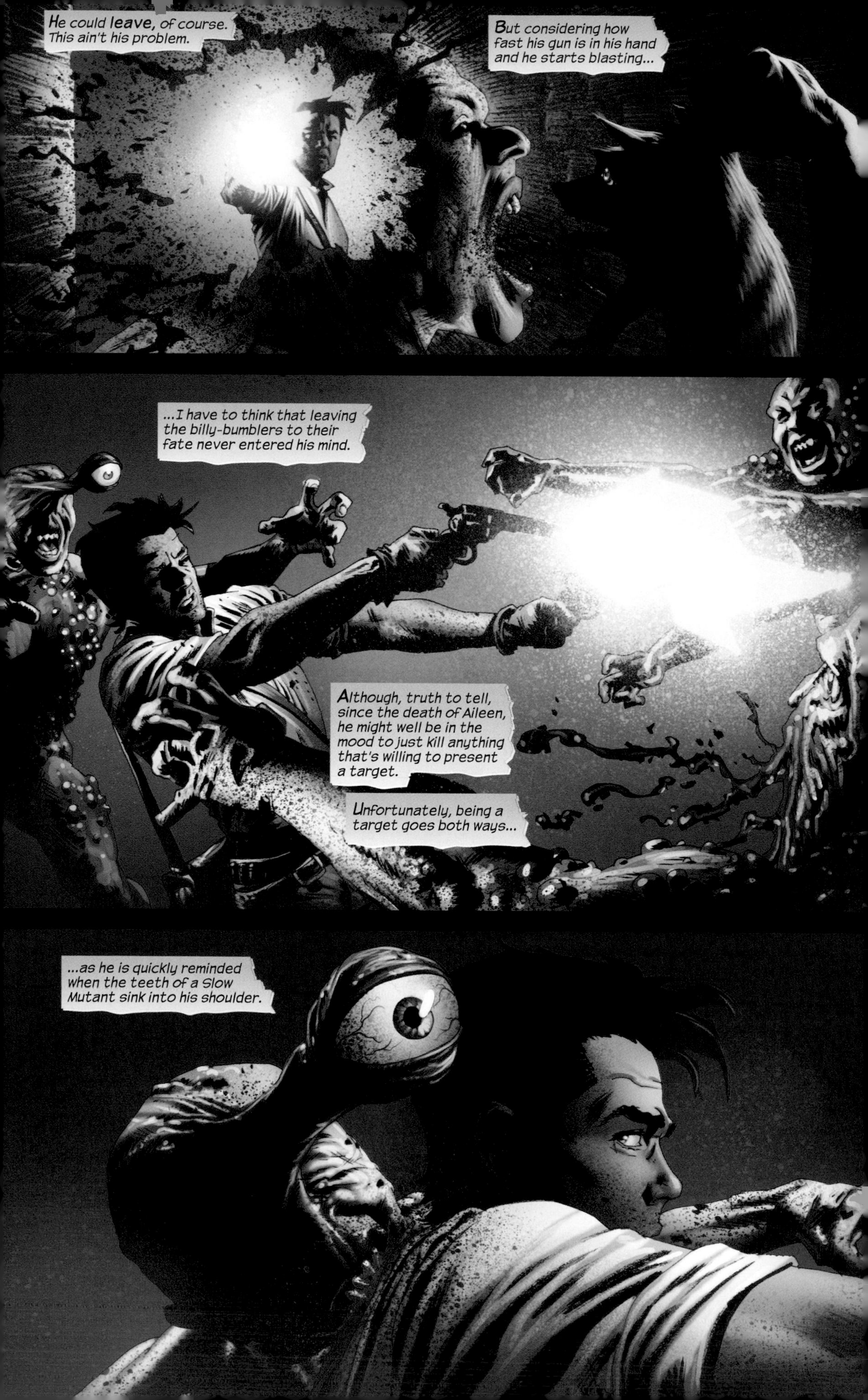
He could leave, of course. This ain't his problem.
But considering how fast his gun is in his hand and he starts blasting...
...I have to think that leaving the billy-bumblers to their fate never entered his mind.
Although, truth to tell, since the death of Aileen, he might well be in the mood to just kill anything that's willing to present a target.
Unfortunately, being a target goes both ways...
...as he is quickly reminded when the teeth of a Slow Mutant sink into his shoulder.

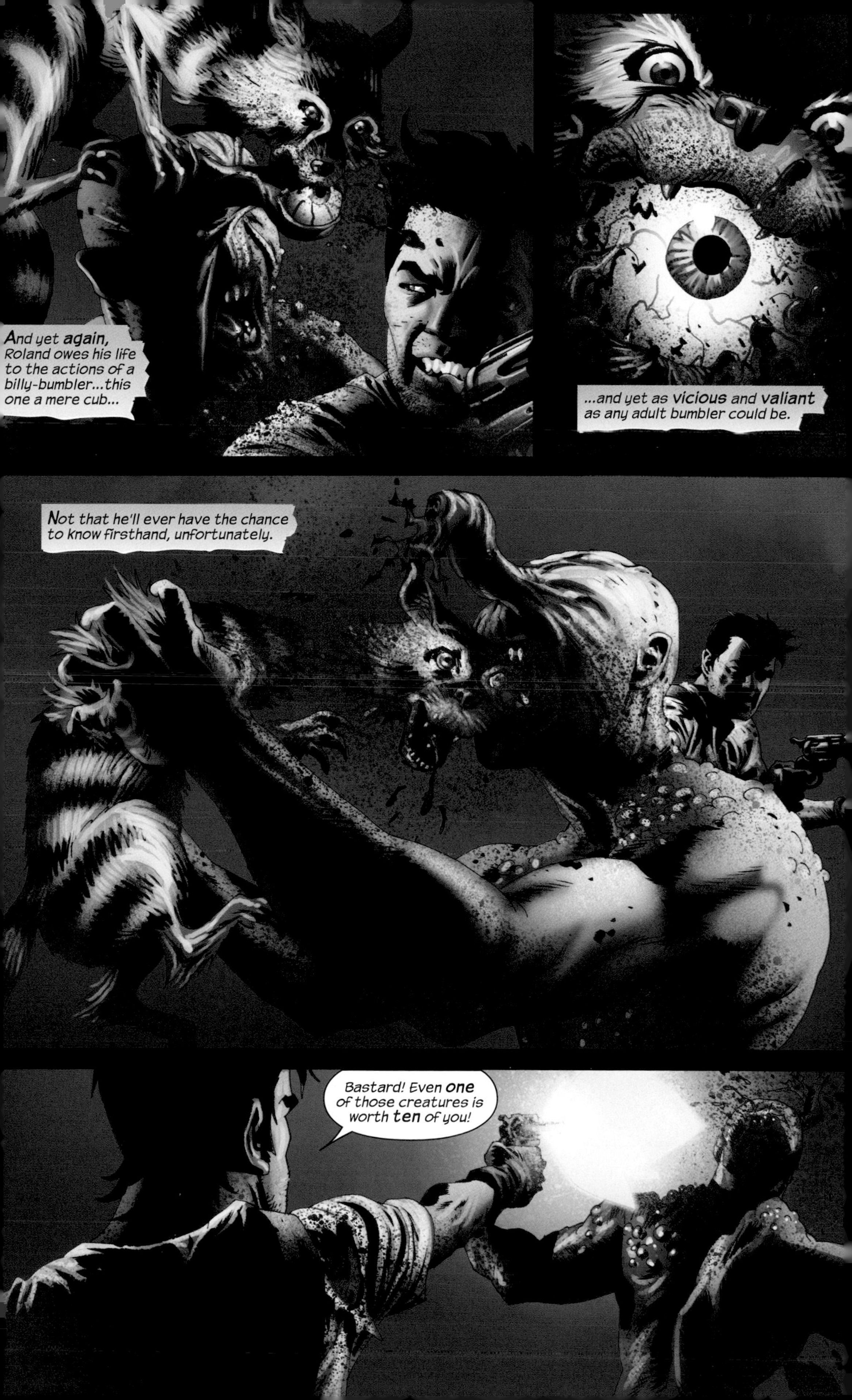
And yet again, Roland owes his life to the actions of a billy-bumbler...this one a mere cub...
...and yet as vicious and valiant as any adult bumbler could be.
Not that he'll ever have the chance to know firsthand, unfortunately.
Bastard! Even one of those creatures is worth ten of you!

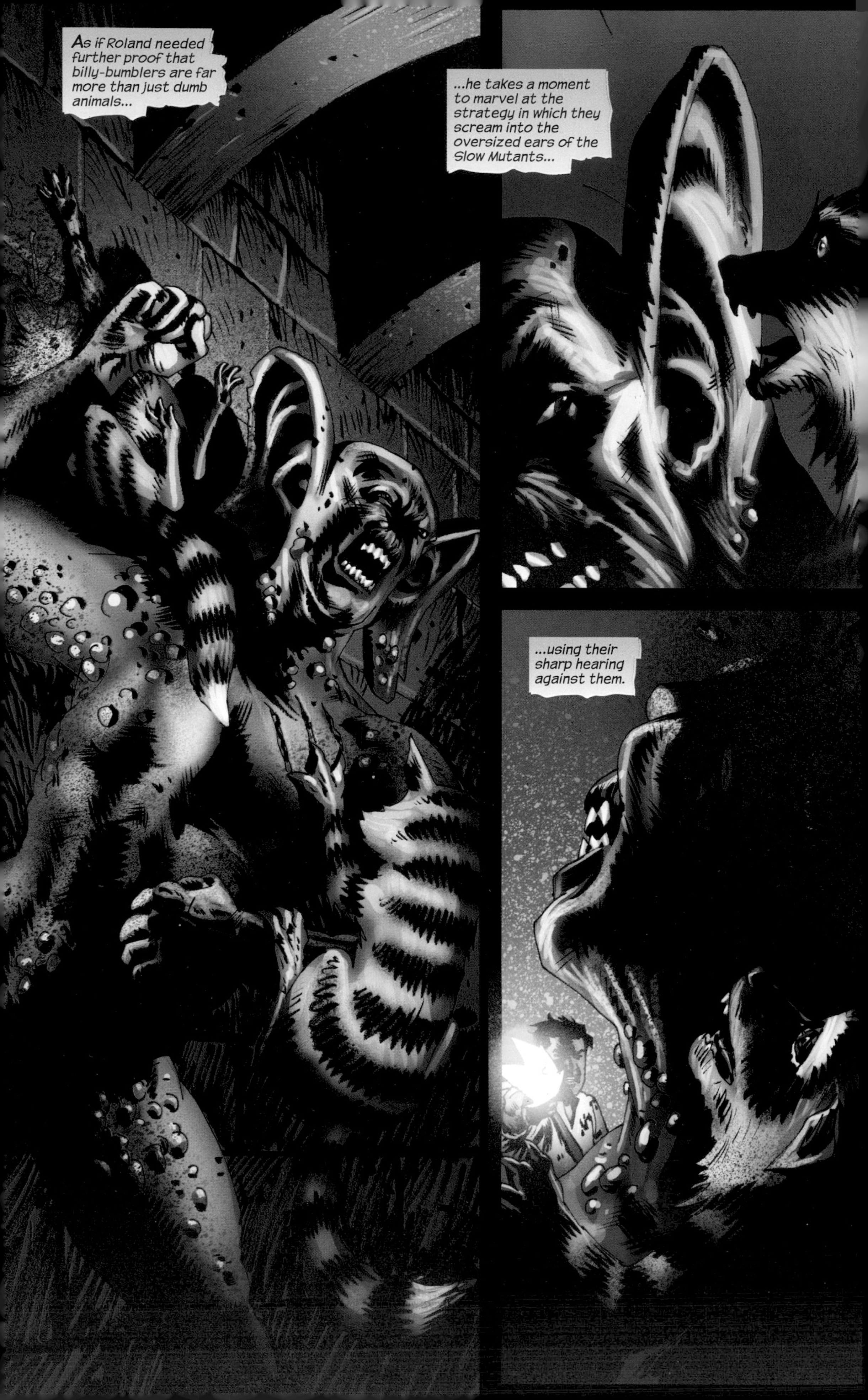
As if Roland needed further proof that billy-bumblers are far more than just dumb animals...
...he takes a moment to marvel at the strategy in which they scream into the oversized ears of the Slow Mutants...
...using their sharp hearing against them.

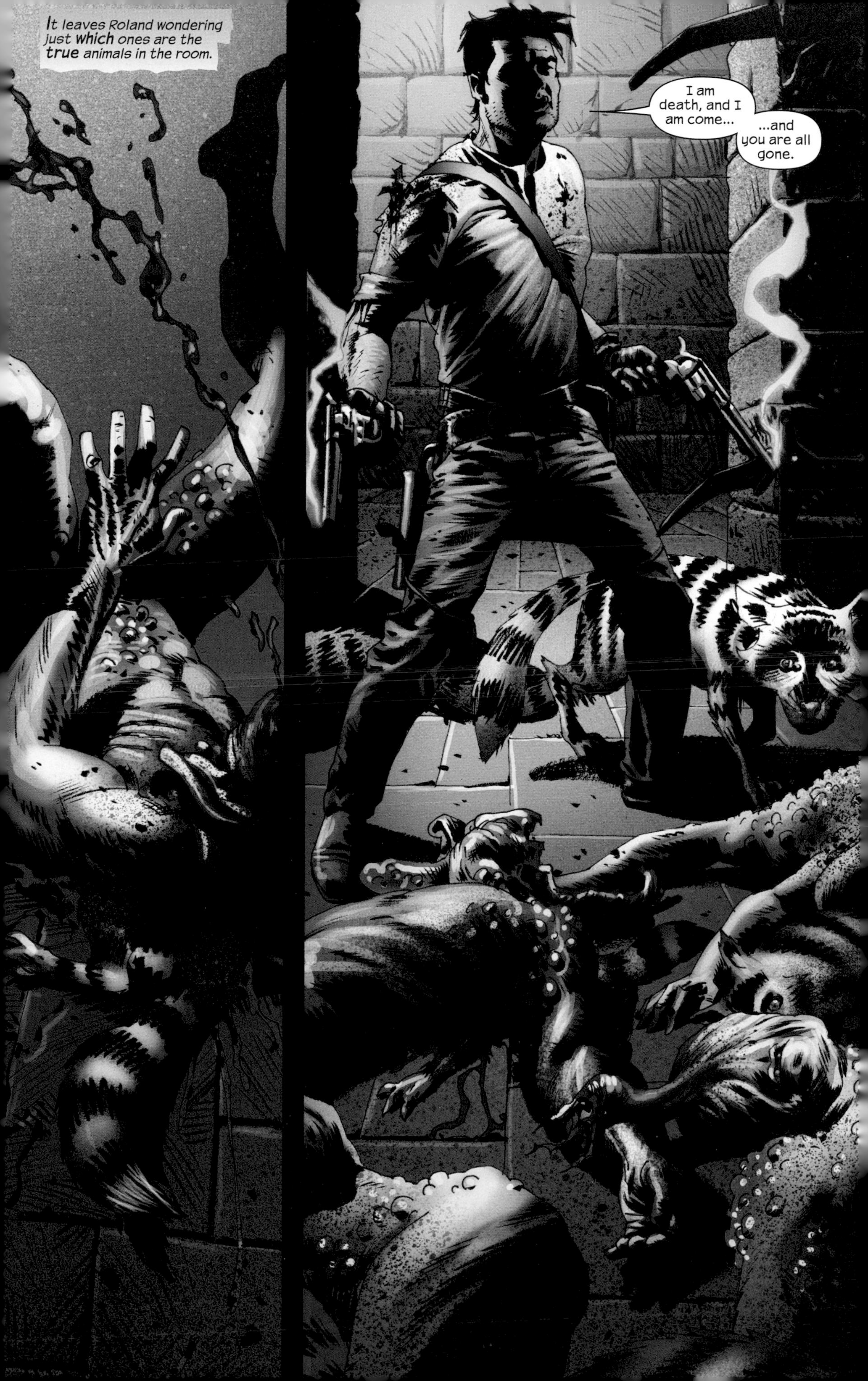
It leaves Roland wondering just **which** ones are the **true** animals in the room.
I am death, and I am come...
...and you are all gone.

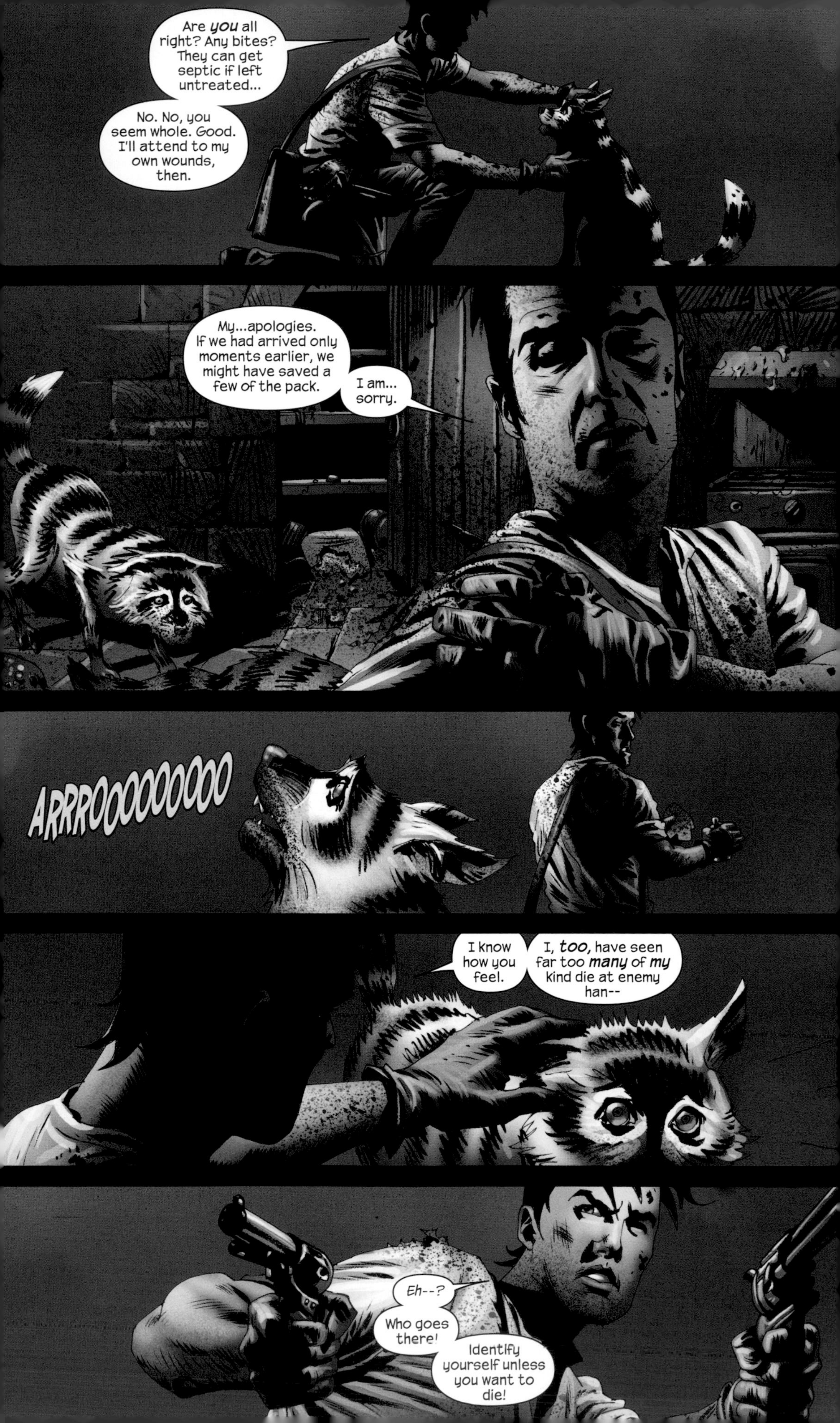

Are *you* all right? Any bites? They can get septic if left untreated...
No. No, you seem whole. Good. I'll attend to my own wounds, then.
My...apologies. If we had arrived only moments earlier, we might have saved a few of the pack.
I am... sorry.
ARRROOOOOOOOO
I know how you feel.
I, *too,* have seen far too *many* of *my* kind die at enemy han--
Eh--?
Who goes there!
Identify yourself unless you want to die!

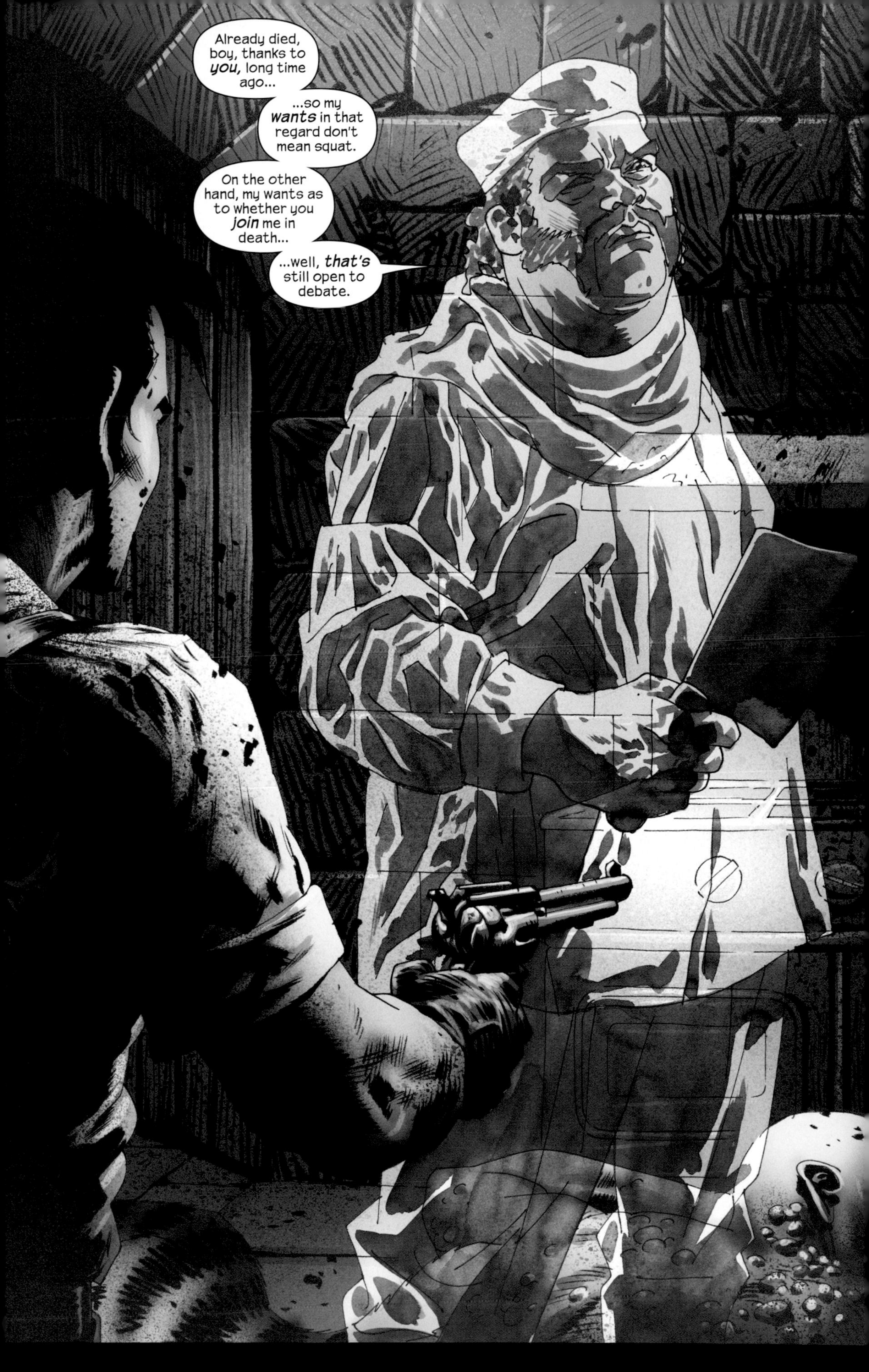
Already died, boy, thanks to *you,* long time ago...
...so my *wants* in that regard don't mean squat.
On the other hand, my wants as to whether you *join* me in death...
...well, *that's* still open to debate.

STEPHEN KING

THE DARK TOWER

~ THE GUNSLINGER ~

THE JOURNEY BEGINS

CHAPTER THREE

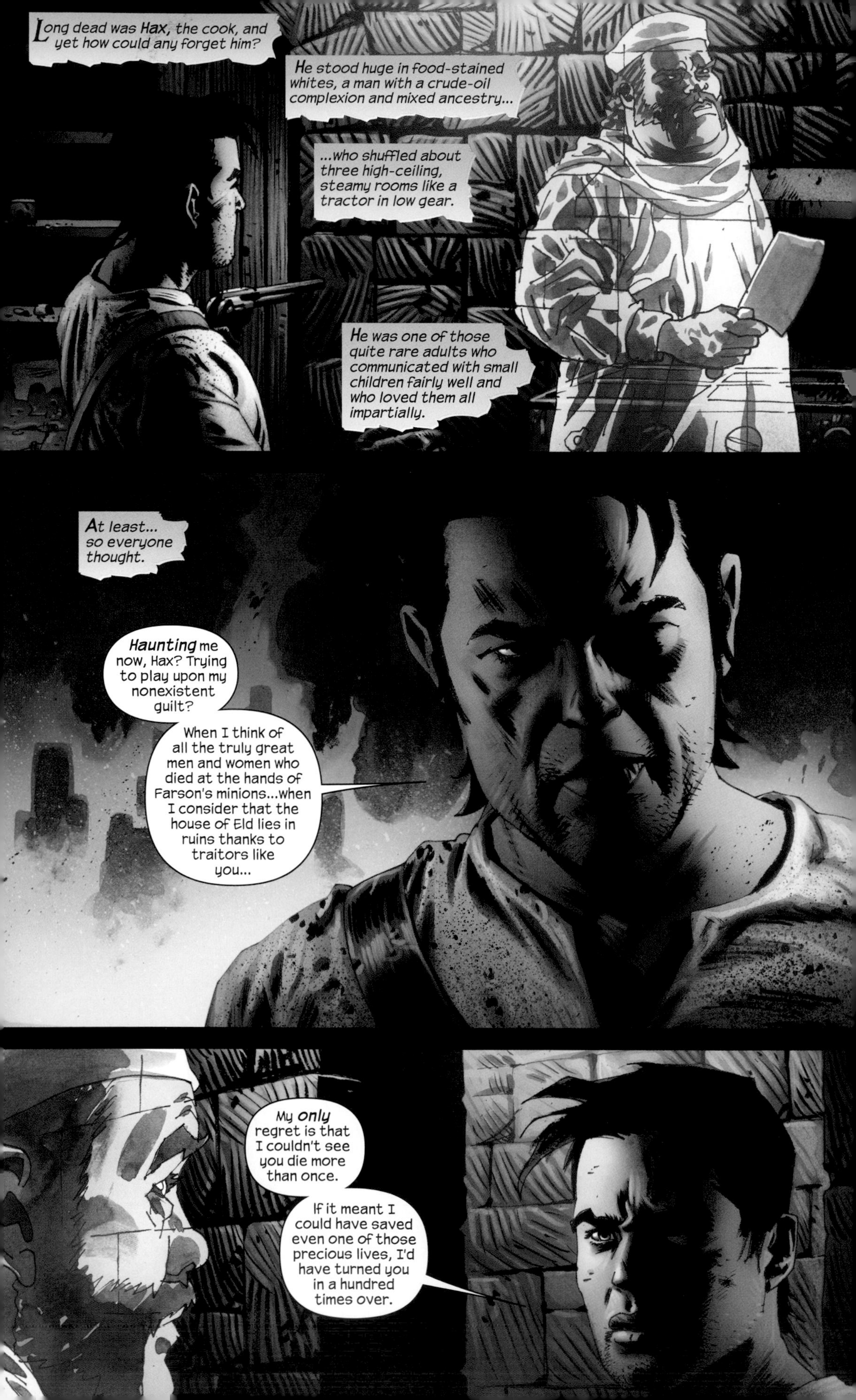
Long dead was Hax, the cook, and yet how could any forget him?
He stood huge in food-stained whites, a man with a crude-oil complexion and mixed ancestry...
...who shuffled about three high-ceiling, steamy rooms like a tractor in low gear.
He was one of those quite rare adults who communicated with small children fairly well and who loved them all impartially.
At least... so everyone thought.
Haunting me now, Hax? Trying to play upon my nonexistent guilt?
When I think of all the truly great men and women who died at the hands of Farson's minions...when I consider that the house of Eld lies in ruins thanks to traitors like you...
My only regret is that I couldn't see you die more than once.
If it meant I could have saved even one of those precious lives, I'd have turned you in a hundred times over.

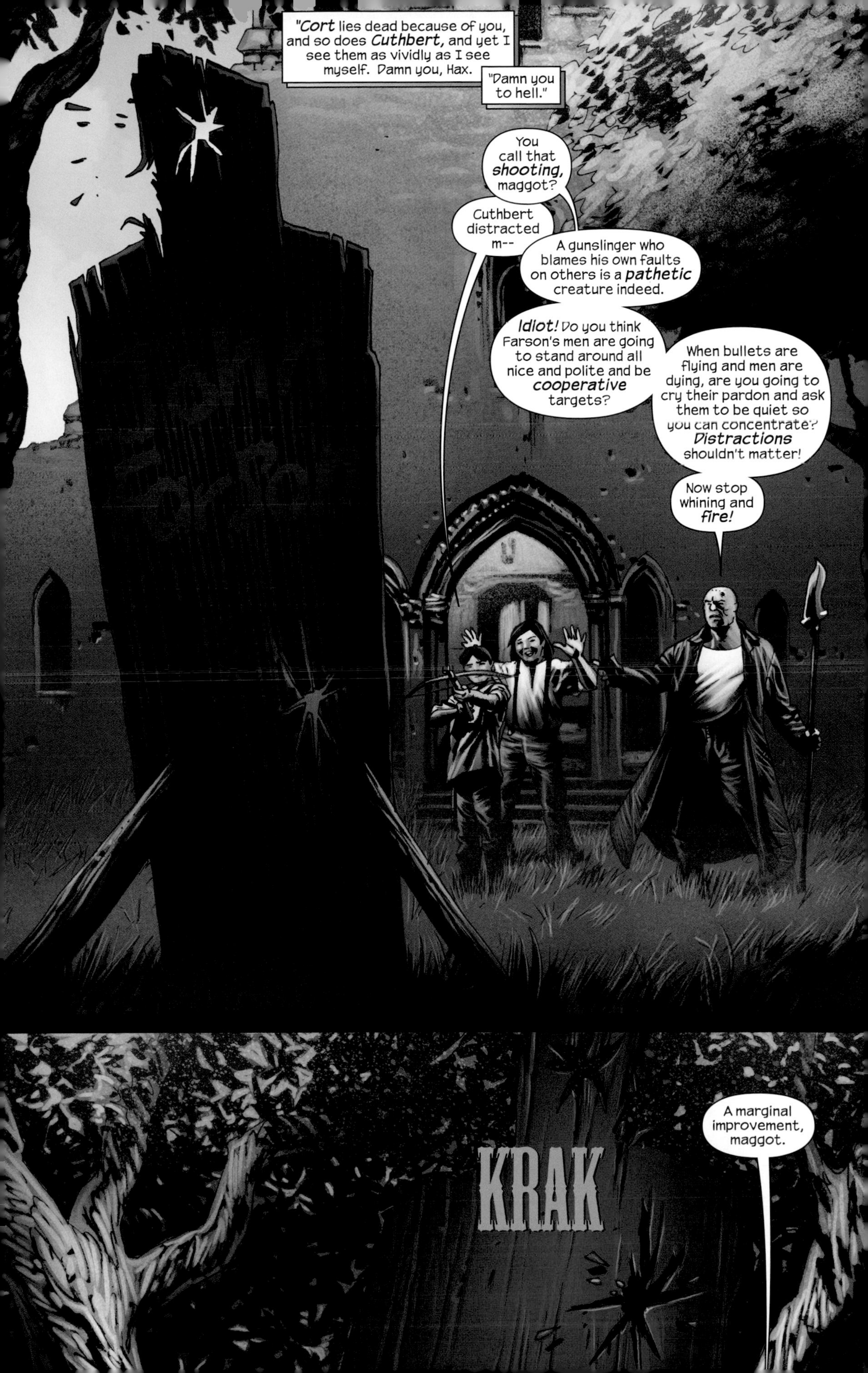
"Cort lies dead because of you, and so does Cuthbert, and yet I see them as vividly as I see myself. Damn you, Hax.
"Damn you to hell."
You call that shooting, maggot?
Cuthbert distracted m--
A gunslinger who blames his own faults on others is a pathetic creature indeed.
Idiot! Do you think Farson's men are going to stand around all nice and polite and be cooperative targets?
When bullets are flying and men are dying, are you going to cry their pardon and ask them to be quiet so you can concentrate? Distractions shouldn't matter!
Now stop whining and fire!
KRAK
A marginal improvement, maggot.

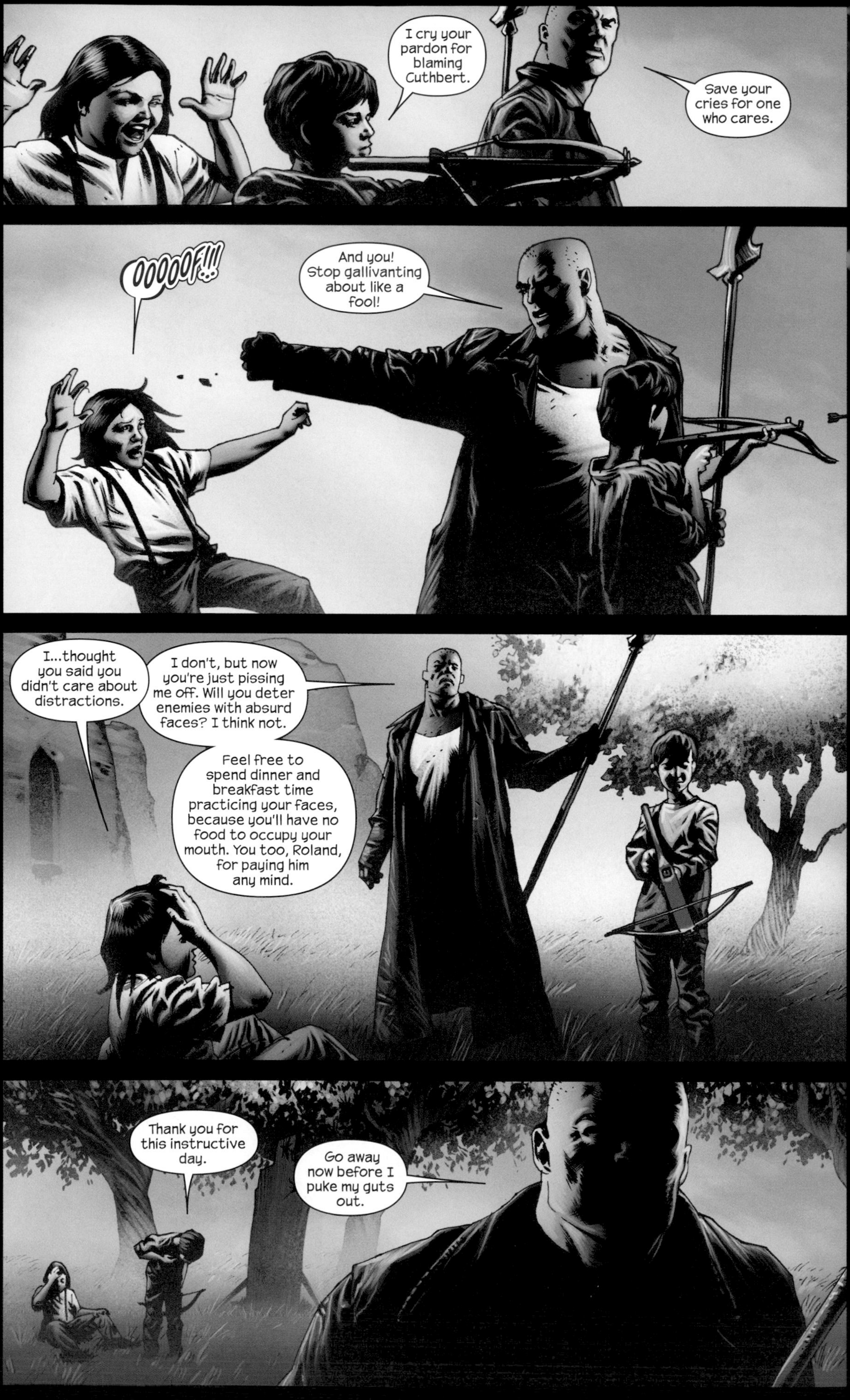
I cry your pardon for blaming Cuthbert.
Save your cries for one who cares.
OOOOOF!!!
And you! Stop gallivanting about like a fool!
I...thought you said you didn't care about distractions.
I don't, but now you're just pissing me off. Will you deter enemies with absurd faces? I think not.
Feel free to spend dinner and breakfast time practicing your faces, because you'll have no food to occupy your mouth. You too, Roland, for paying him any mind.
Thank you for this instructive day.
Go away now before I puke my guts out.

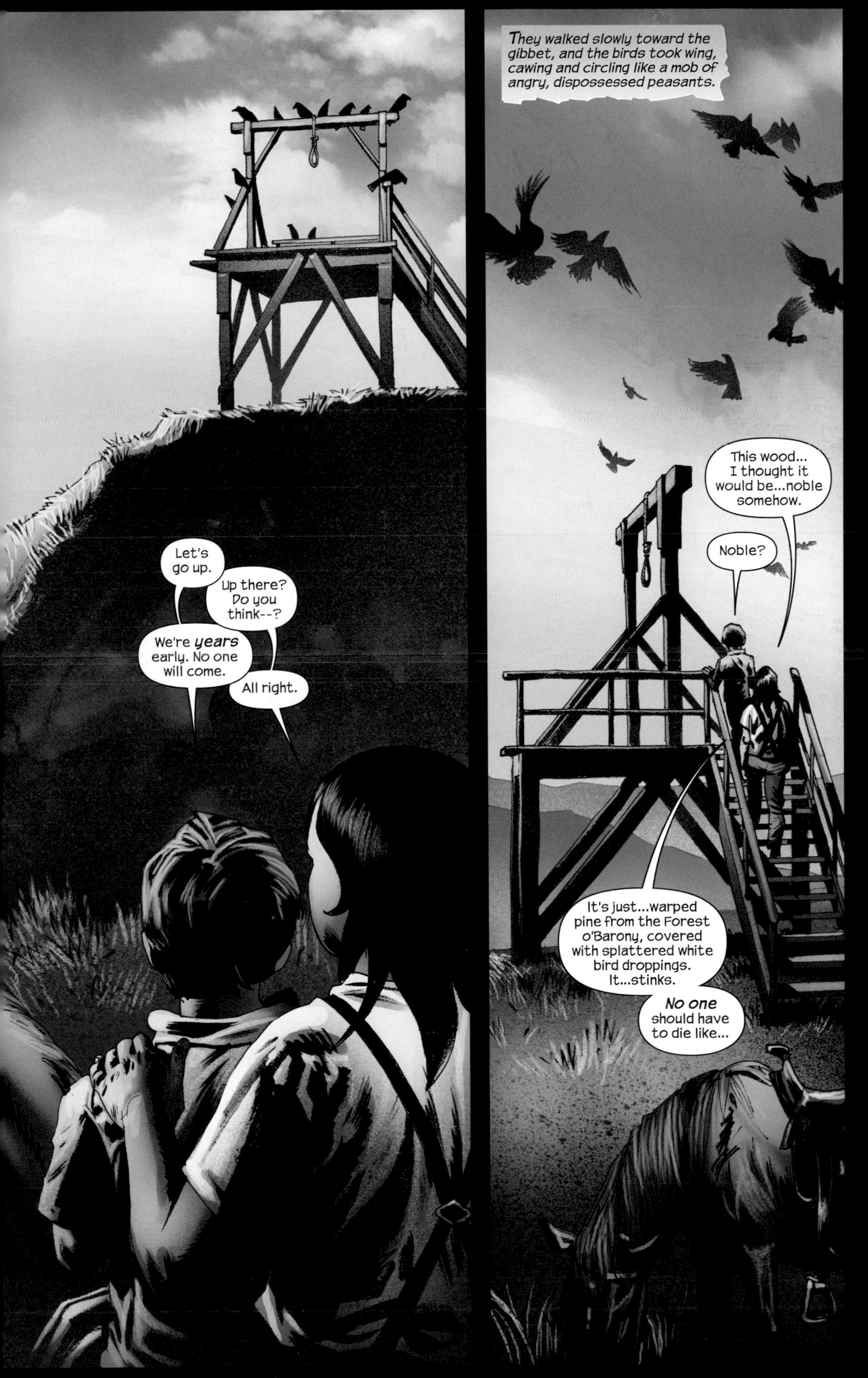
Let's go up.
Up there? Do you think--?
We're *years* early. No one will come.
All right.
They walked slowly toward the gibbet, and the birds took wing, cawing and circling like a mob of angry, dispossessed peasants.
This wood... I thought it would be...noble somehow.
Noble?
It's just...warped pine from the Forest O'Barony, covered with splattered white bird droppings. It...stinks.
No one should have to die like...

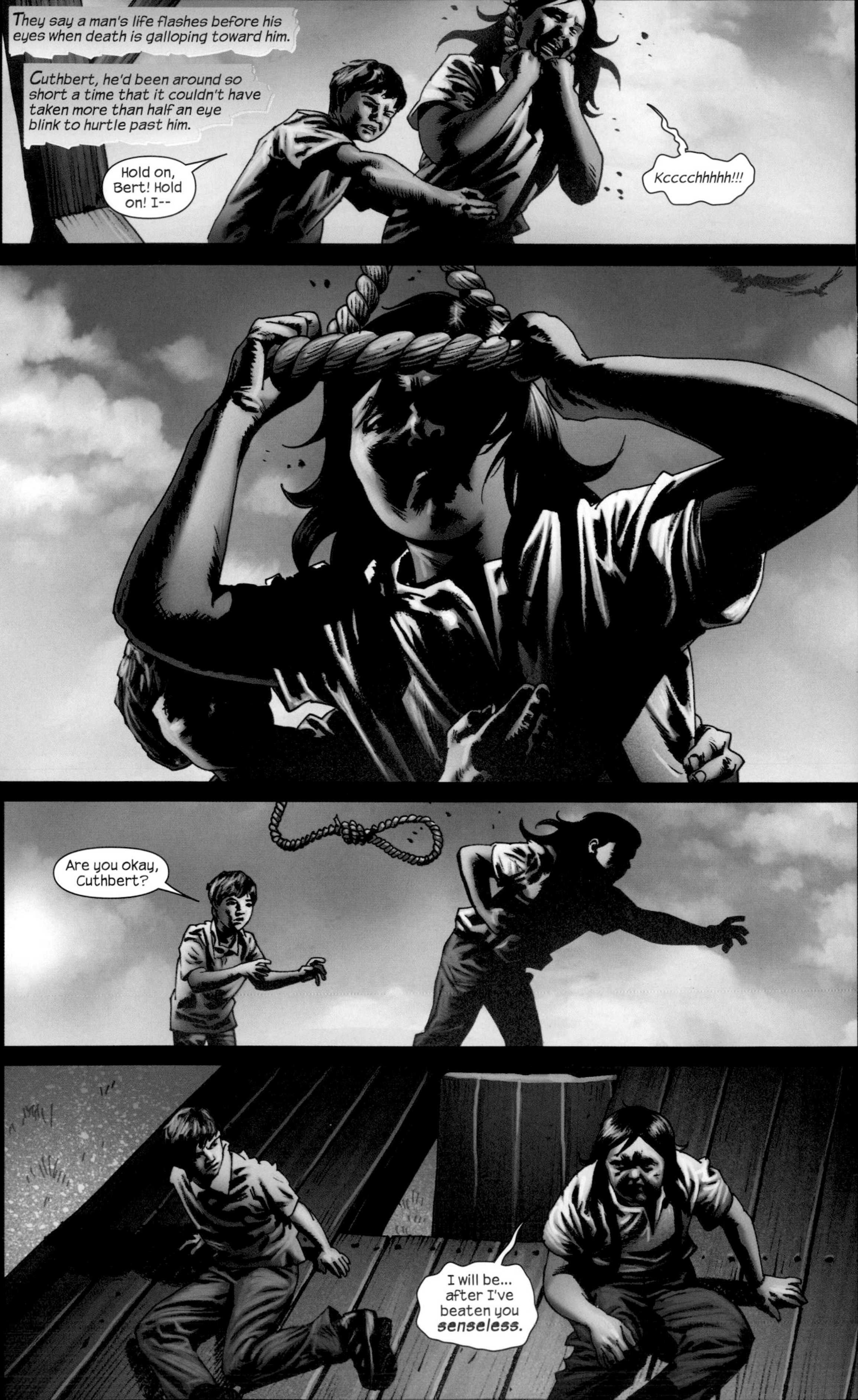
They say a man's life flashes before his eyes when death is galloping toward him.
Cuthbert, he'd been around so short a time that it couldn't have taken more than half an eye blink to hurtle past him.
Hold on, Bert! Hold on! I--
Kccccchhhhh!!!
Are you okay, Cuthbert?
I will be... after I've beaten you **senseless.**

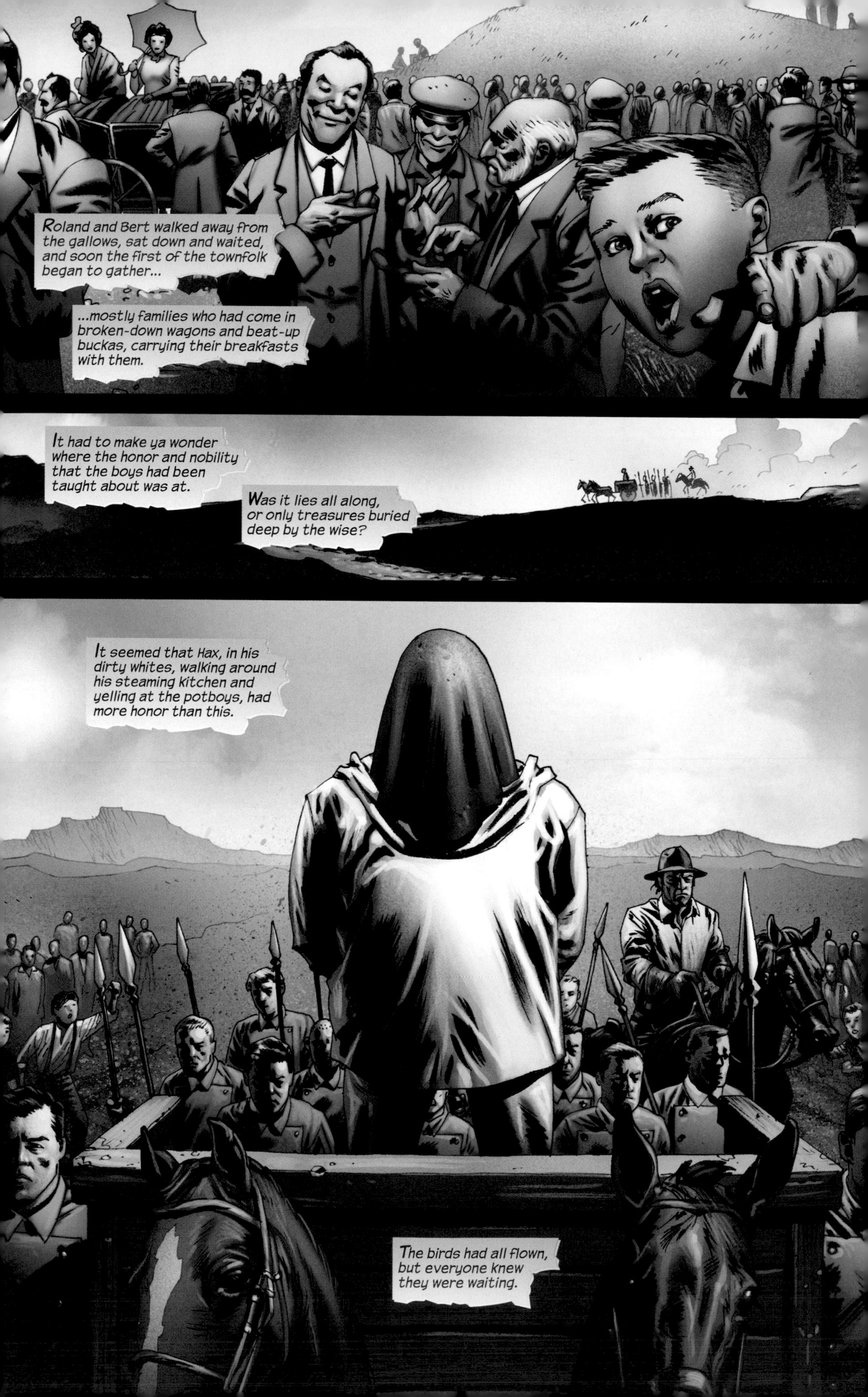

Roland and Bert walked away from the gallows, sat down and waited, and soon the first of the townfolk began to gather...
...mostly families who had come in broken-down wagons and beat-up buckas, carrying their breakfasts with them.
It had to make ya wonder where the honor and nobility that the boys had been taught about was at.
Was it lies all along, or only treasures buried deep by the wise?
It seemed that Hax, in his dirty whites, walking around his steaming kitchen and yelling at the potboys, had more honor than this.
The birds had all flown, but everyone knew they were waiting.

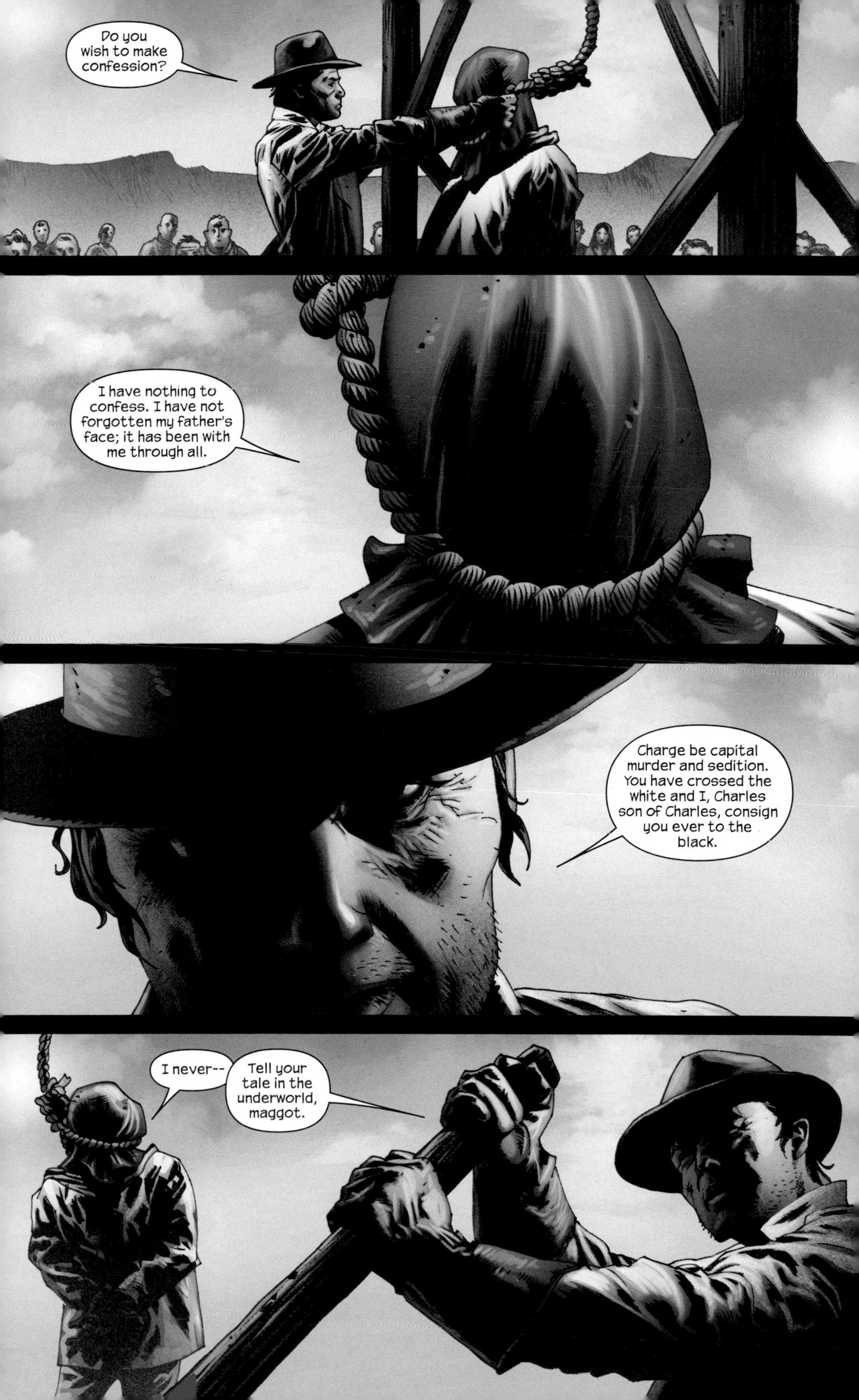
Do you wish to make confession?
I have nothing to confess. I have not forgotten my father's face; it has been with me through all.
Charge be capital murder and sedition. You have crossed the white and I, Charles son of Charles, consign you ever to the black.
I never--
Tell your tale in the underworld, maggot.

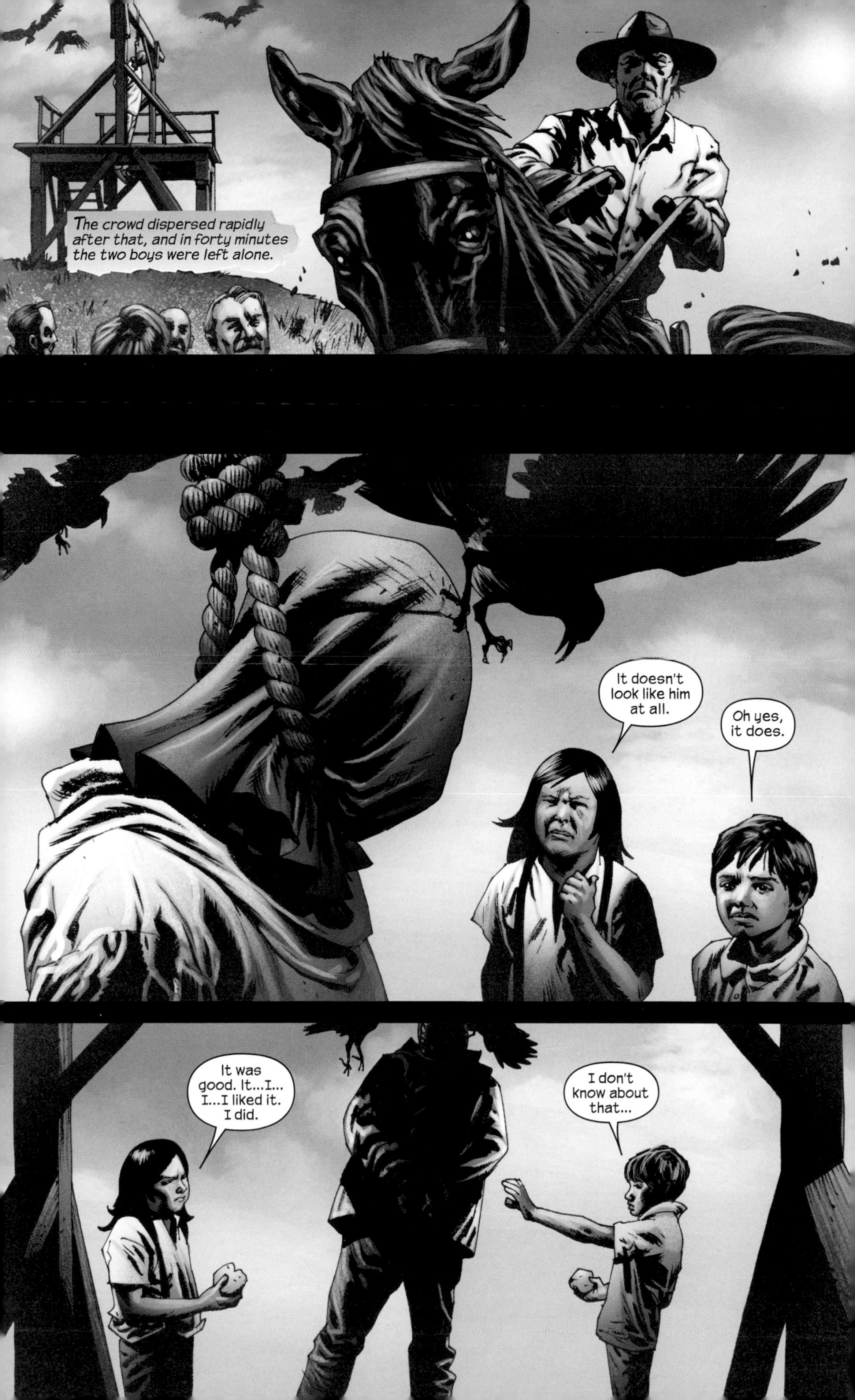
The crowd dispersed rapidly after that, and in forty minutes the two boys were left alone.
It doesn't look like him at all.
Oh yes, it does.
It was good. It...I... I...I liked it. I did.
I don't know about that...

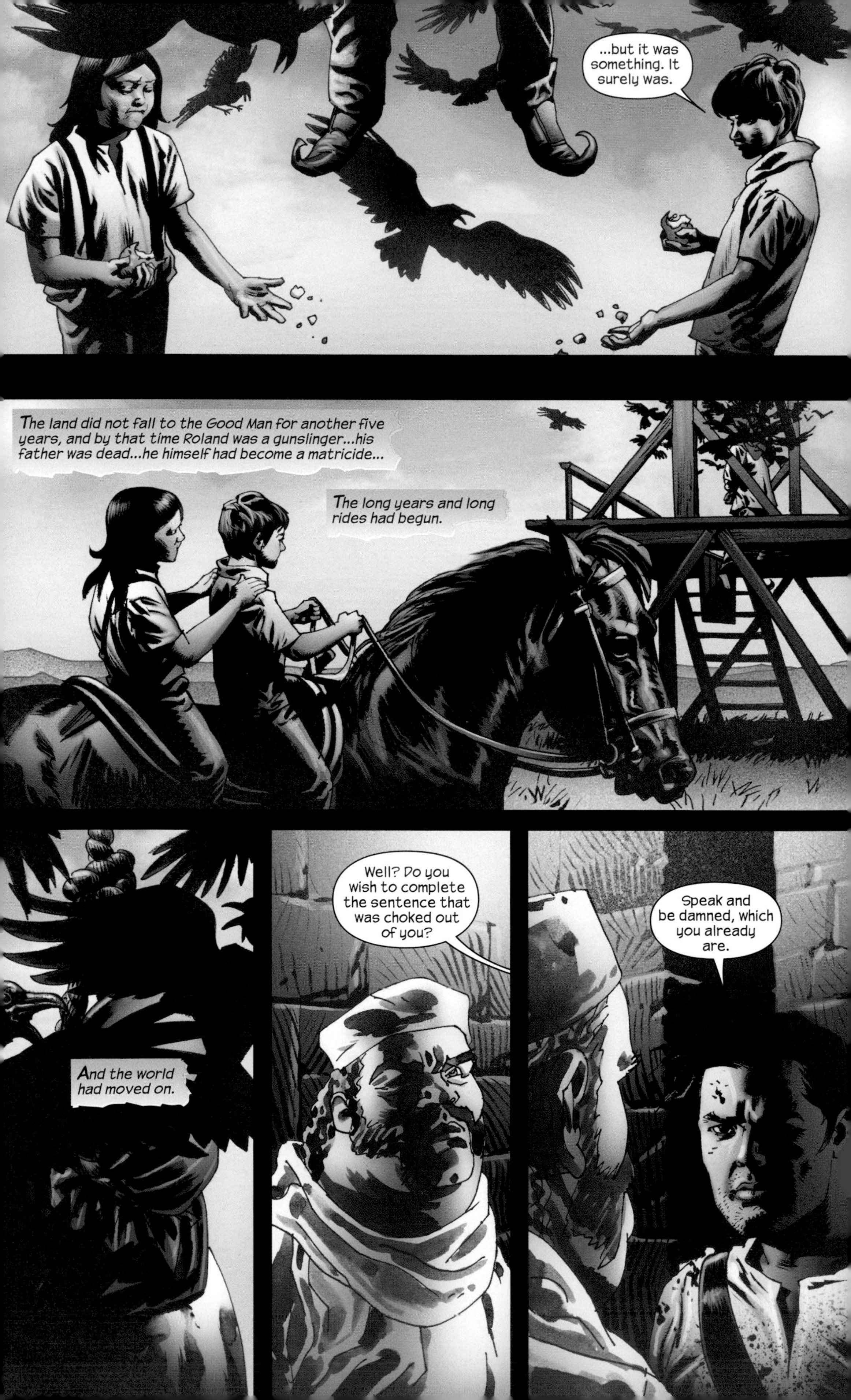
...but it was something. It surely was.
The land did not fall to the Good Man for another five years, and by that time Roland was a gunslinger...his father was dead...he himself had become a matricide...
The long years and long rides had begun.
And the world had moved on.
Well? Do you wish to complete the sentence that was choked out of you?
Speak and be damned, which you already are.

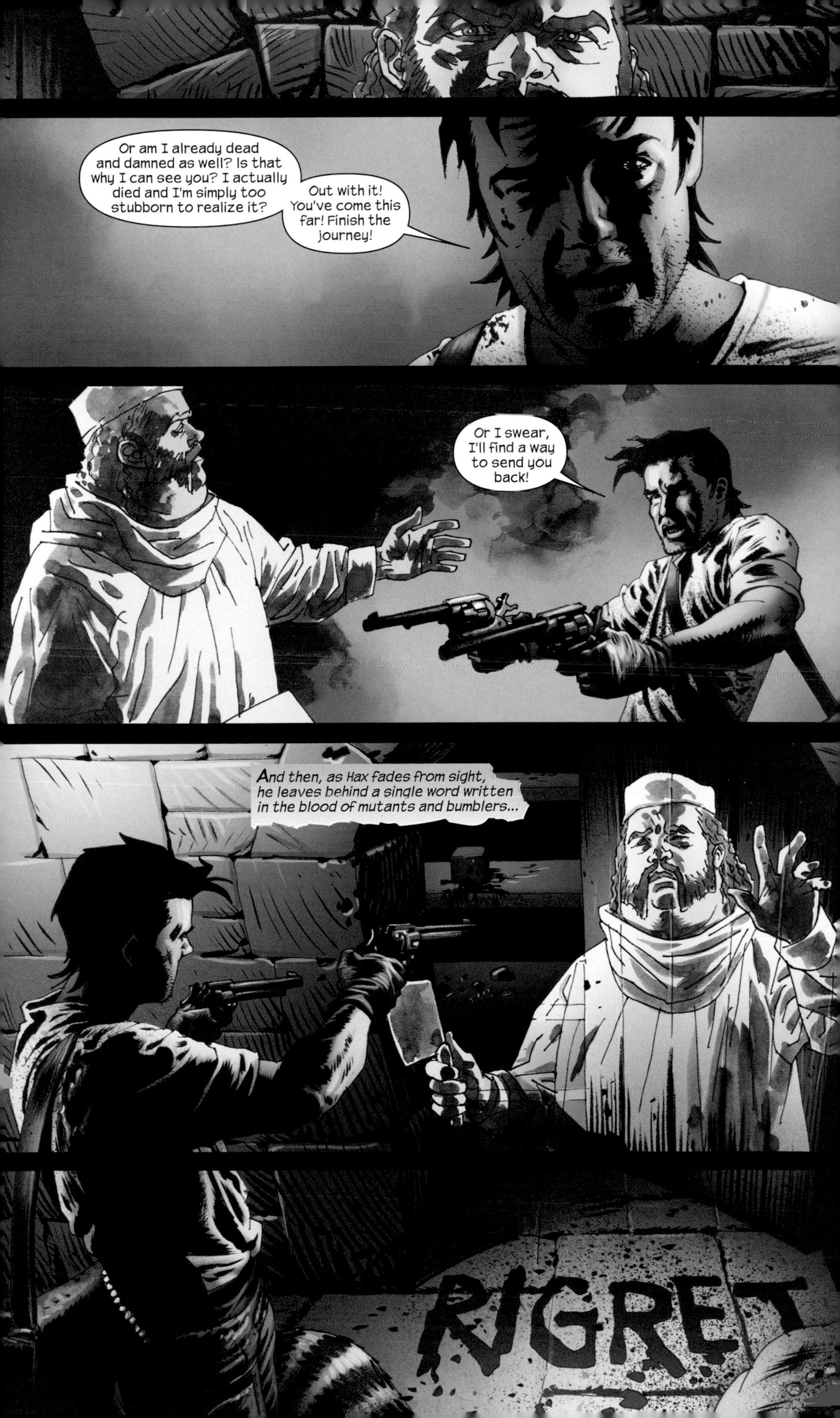

Or am I already dead and damned as well? Is that why I can see you? I actually died and I'm simply too stubborn to realize it?
Out with it! You've come this far! Finish the journey!
Or I swear, I'll find a way to send you back!
And then, as Hax fades from sight, he leaves behind a single word written in the blood of mutants and bumblers...
RIGRET

STEPHEN KING

THE DARK TOWER
~ THE GUNSLINGER ~

THE JOURNEY BEGINS
CHAPTER FOUR

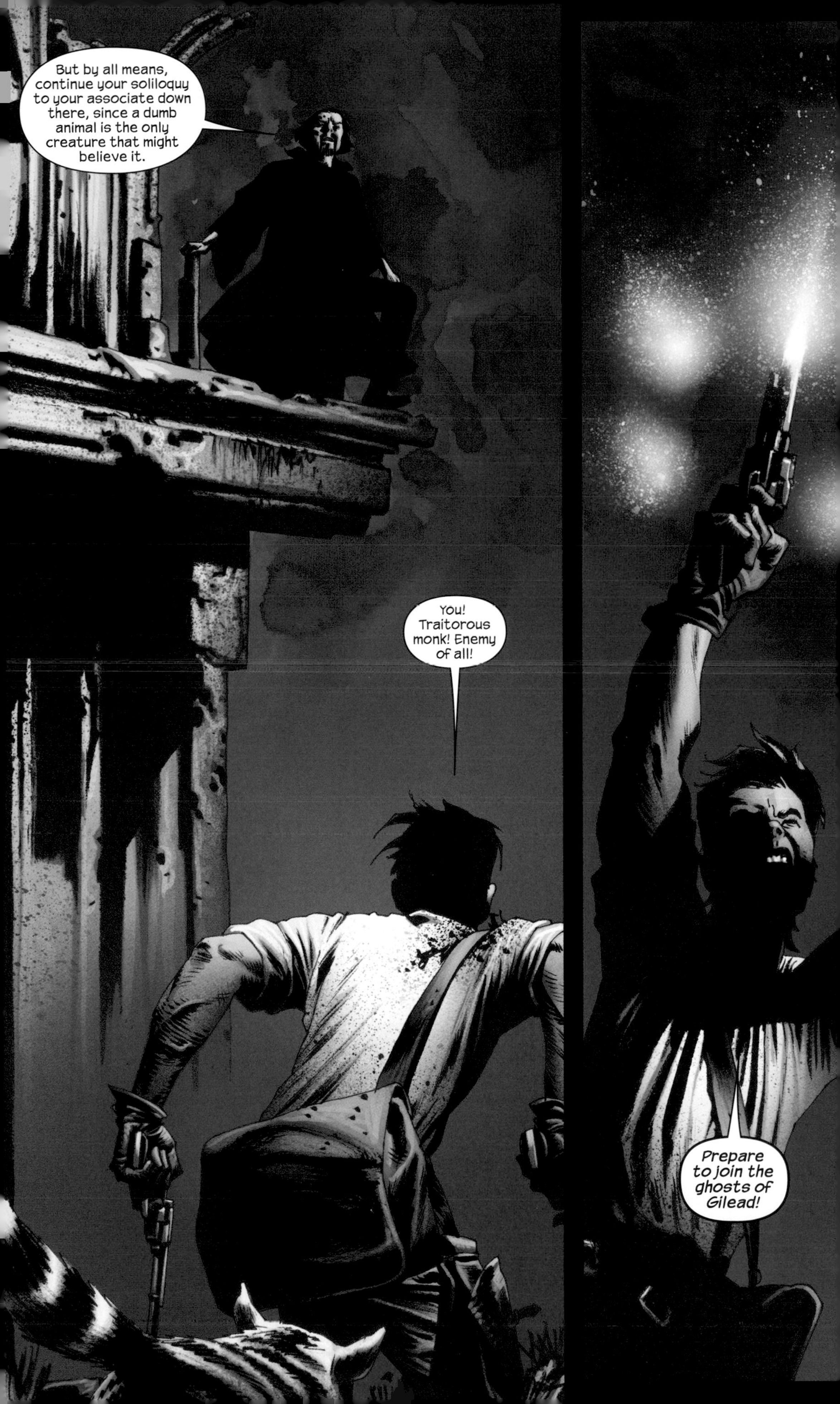
But by all means, continue your soliloquy to your associate down there, since a dumb animal is the only creature that might believe it.
You! Traitorous monk! Enemy of all!
Prepare to join the ghosts of Gilead!

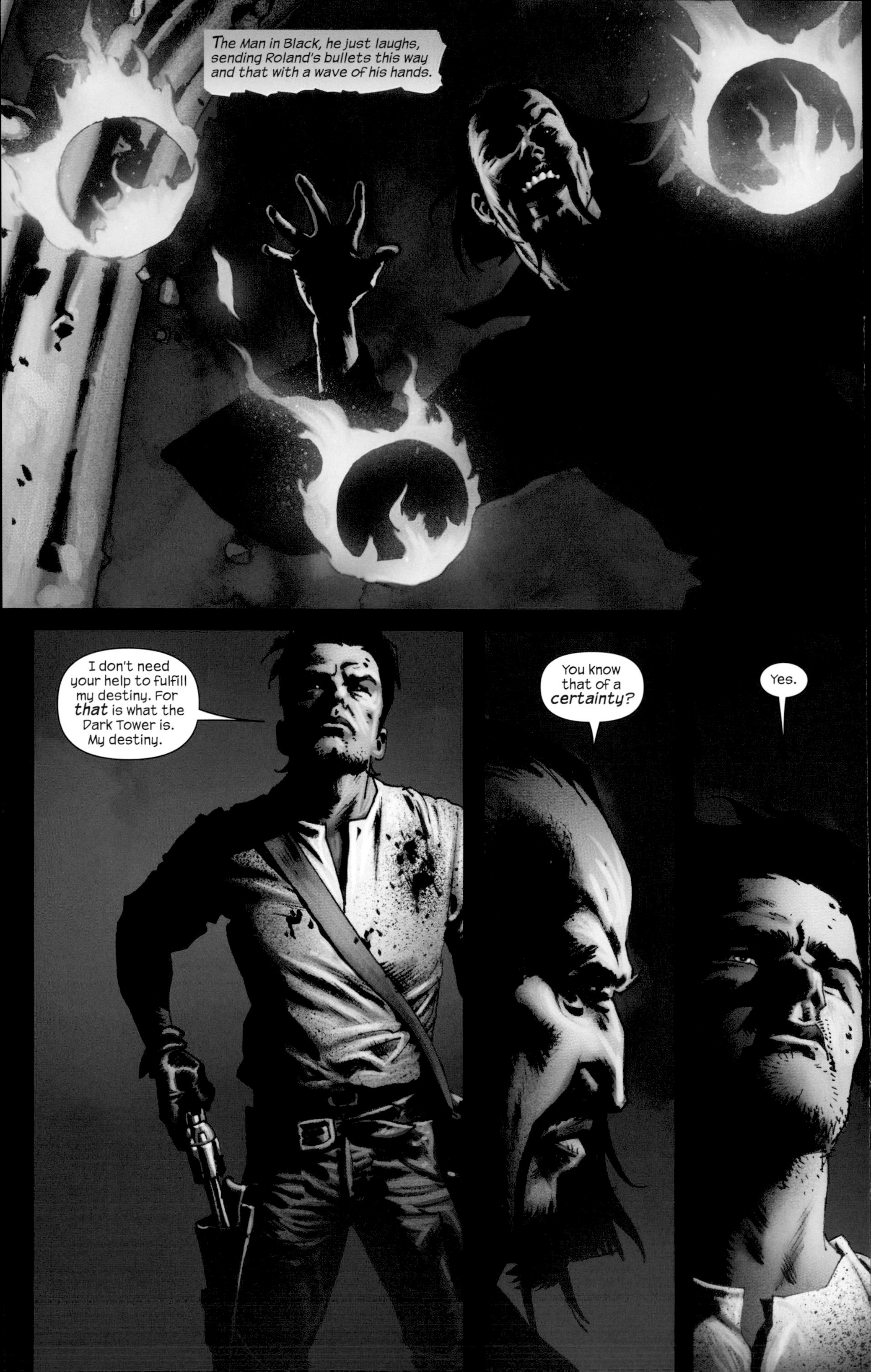

The Man in Black, he just laughs, sending Roland's bullets this way and that with a wave of his hands.
I don't need your help to fulfill my destiny. For *that* is what the Dark Tower is. My destiny.
You know that of a *certainty*?
Yes.

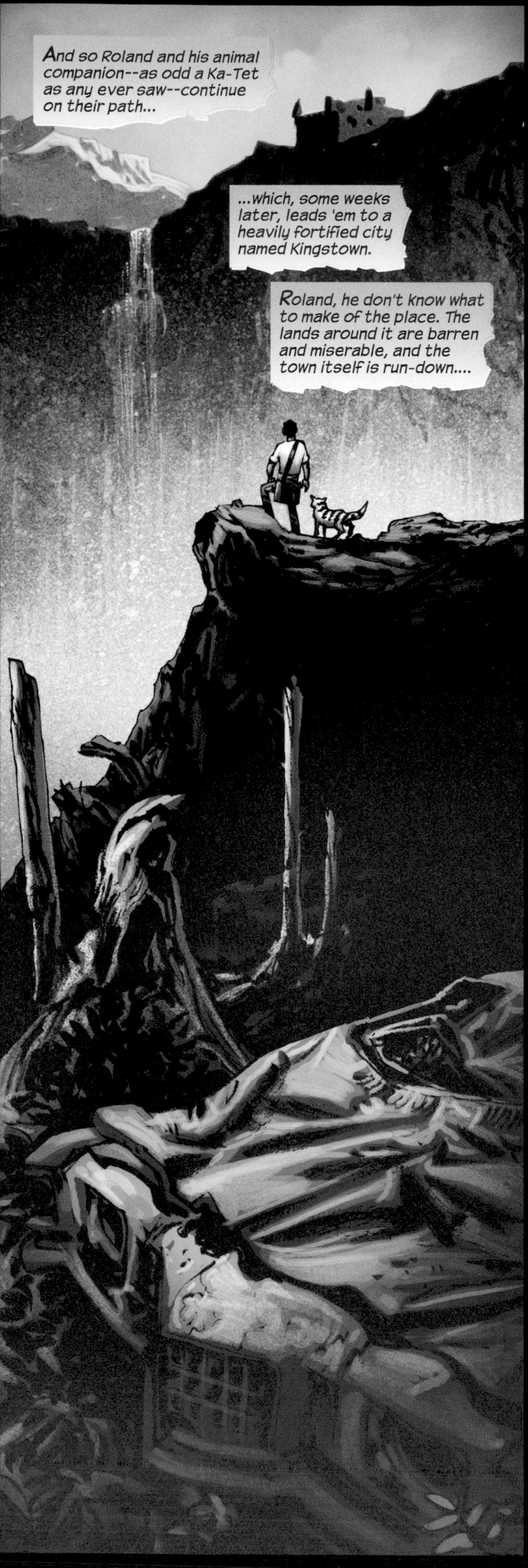
And so Roland and his animal companion--as odd a Ka-Tet as any ever saw--continue on their path...
...which, some weeks later, leads 'em to a heavily fortified city named Kingstown.
Roland, he don't know what to make of the place. The lands around it are barren and miserable, and the town itself is run-down....
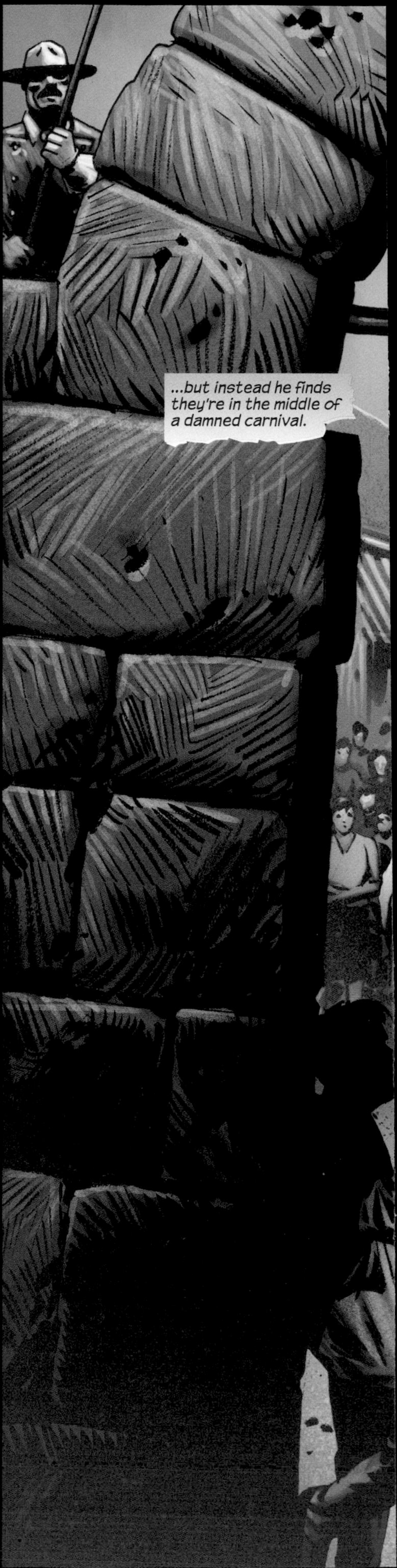
...but instead he finds they're in the middle of a damned carnival.

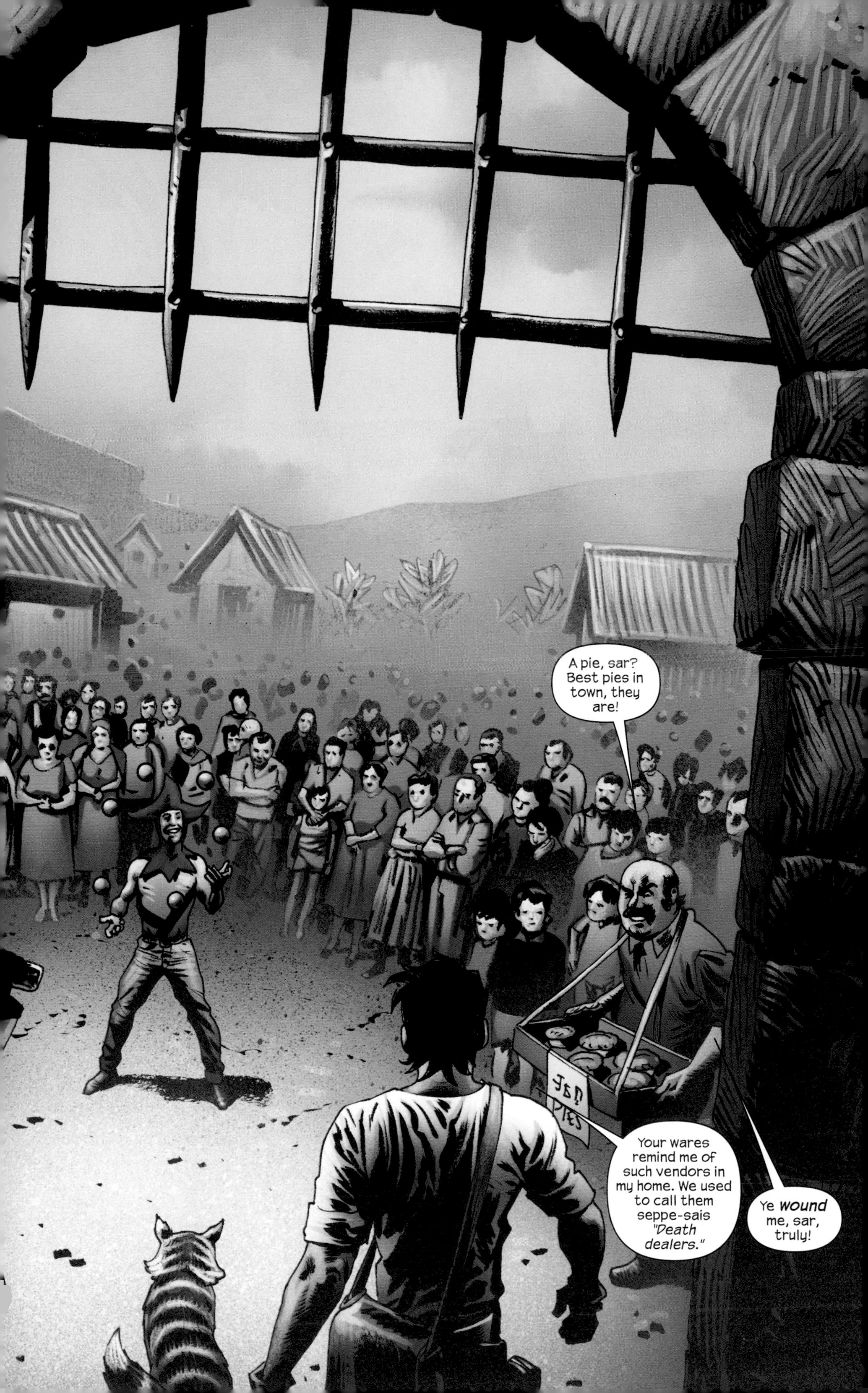
A pie, sar? Best pies in town, they are!
Your wares remind me of such vendors in my home. We used to call them seppe-sais "Death dealers."
Ye *wound* me, sar, truly!

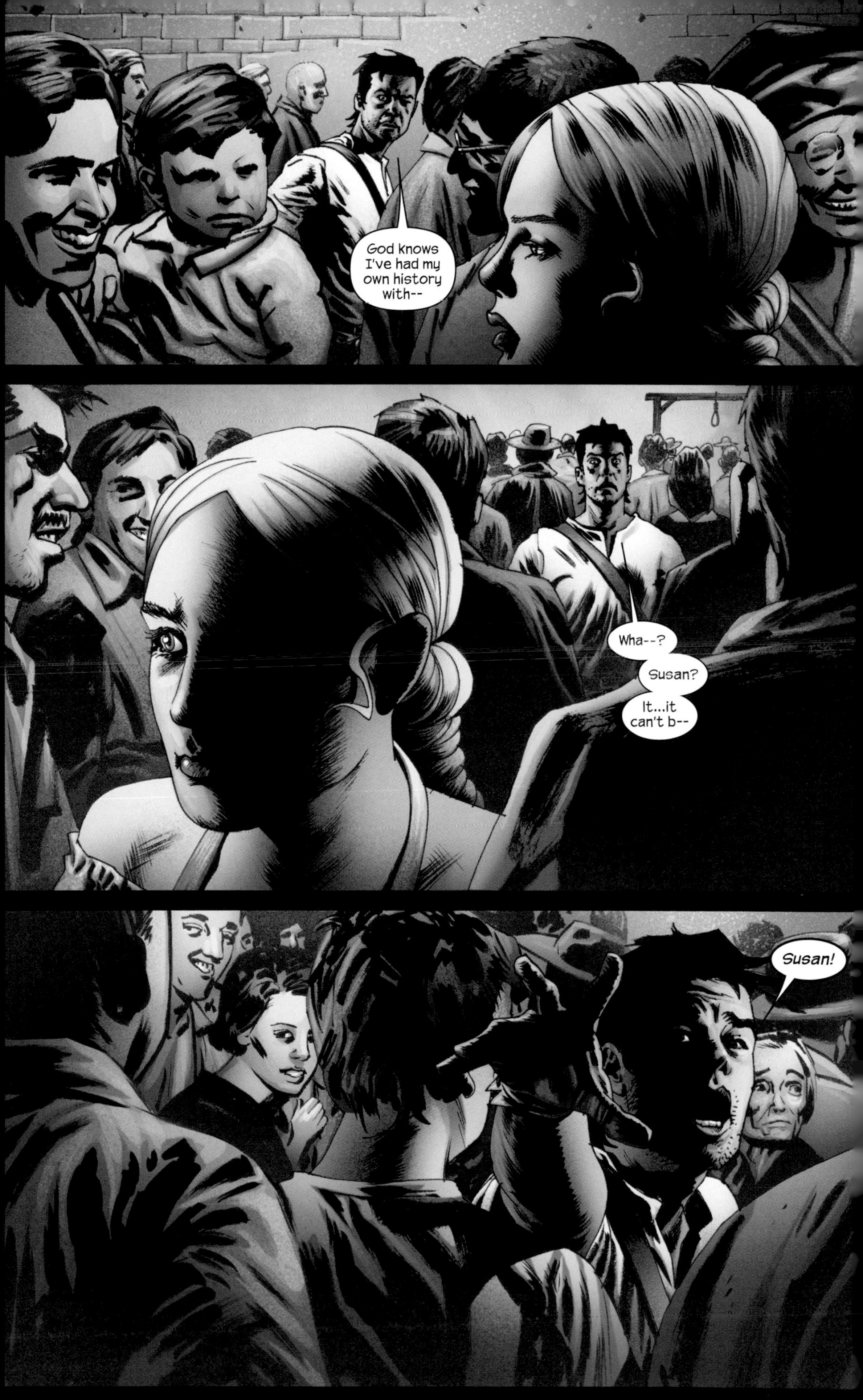
God knows I've had my own history with--
Wha--?
Susan?
It...it can't b--
Susan!

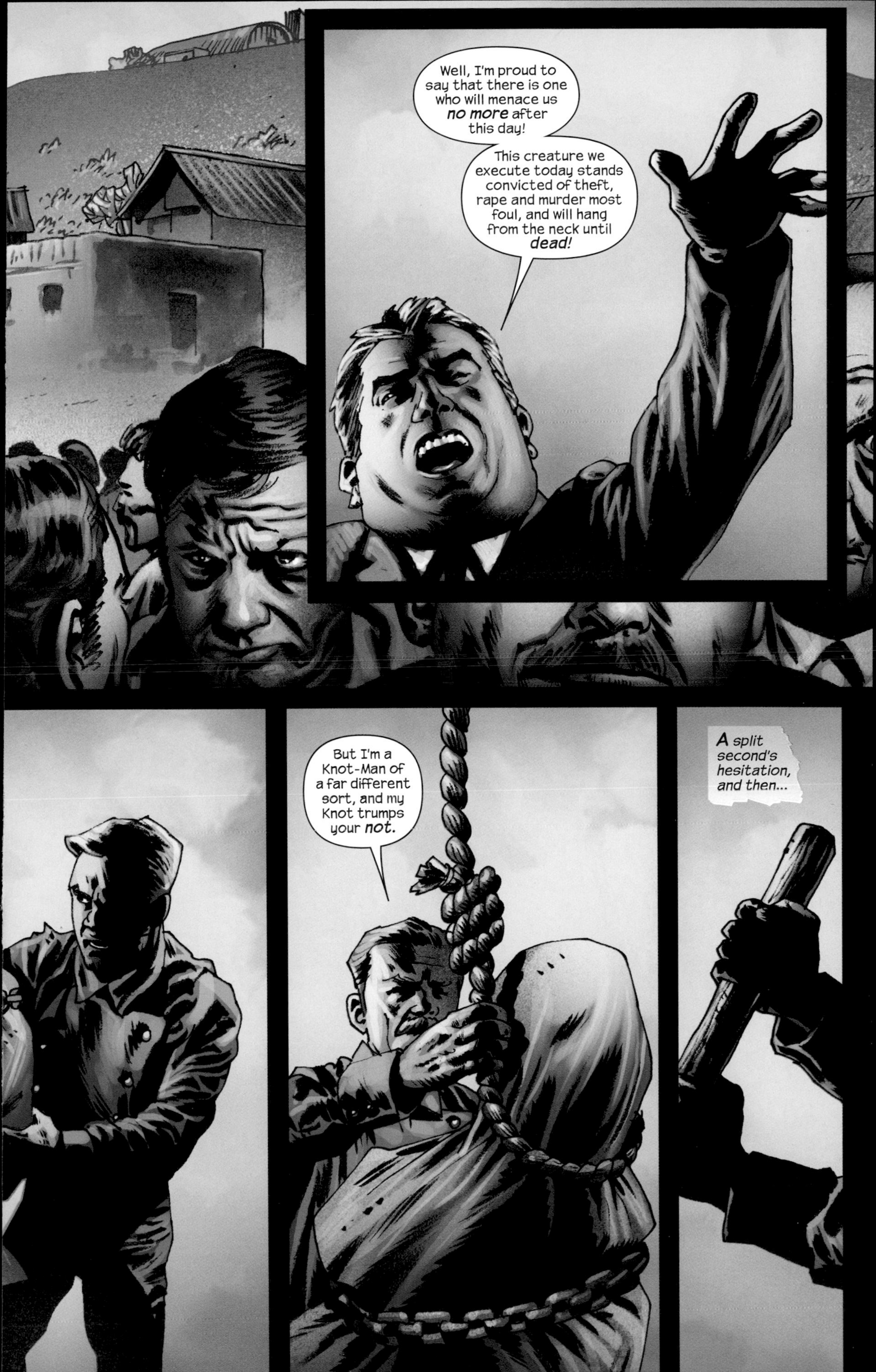

Well, I'm proud to say that there is one who will menace us *no more* after this day!
This creature we execute today stands convicted of theft, rape and murder most foul, and will hang from the neck until *dead!*
But I'm a Knot-Man of a far different sort, and my Knot trumps your *not.*
A split second's hesitation, and then...

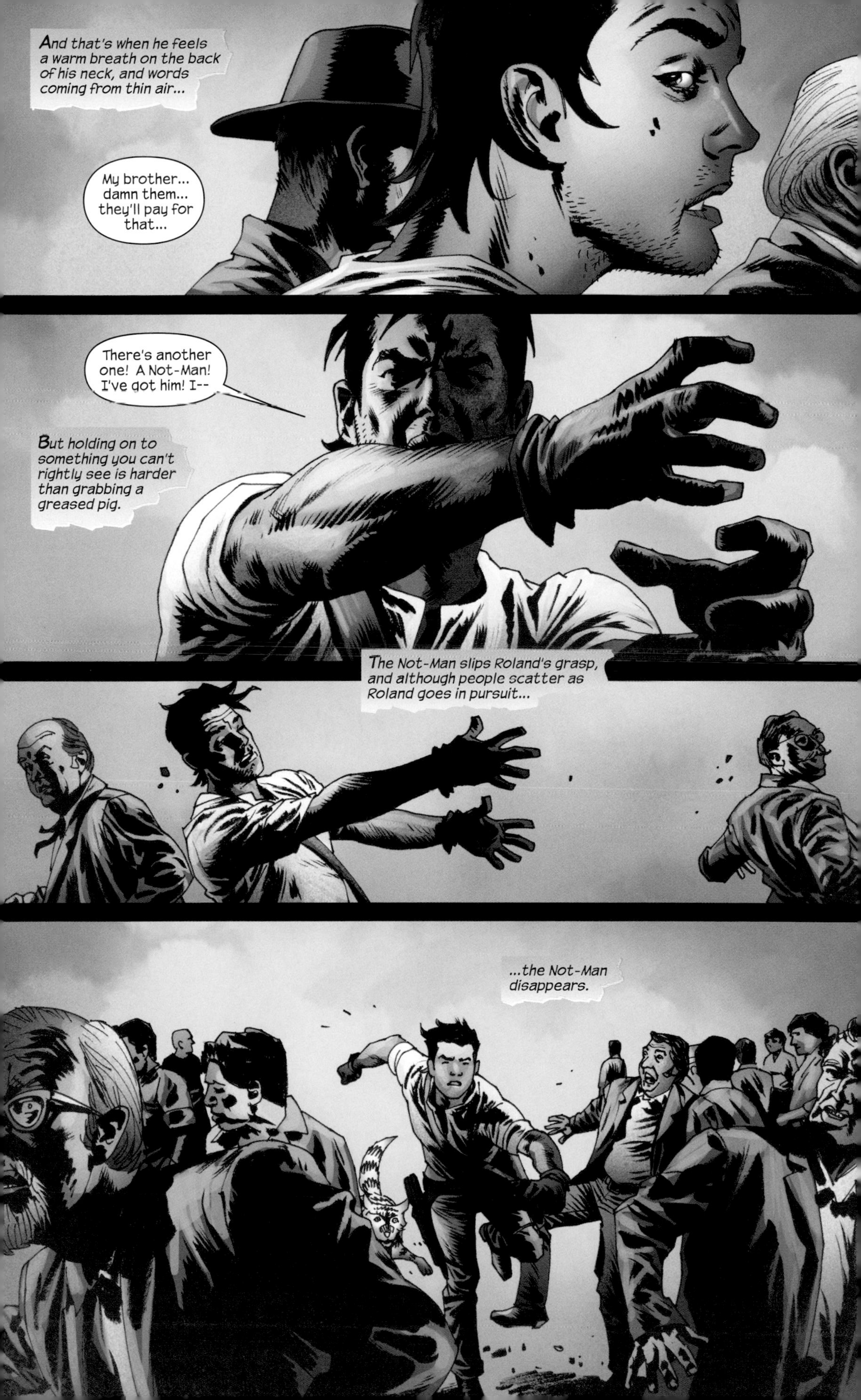
And that's when he feels a warm breath on the back of his neck, and words coming from thin air...
My brother... damn them... they'll pay for that...
There's another one! A Not-Man! I've got him! I--
But holding on to something you can't rightly see is harder than grabbing a greased pig.
The Not-Man slips Roland's grasp, and although people scatter as Roland goes in pursuit...
...the Not-Man disappears.

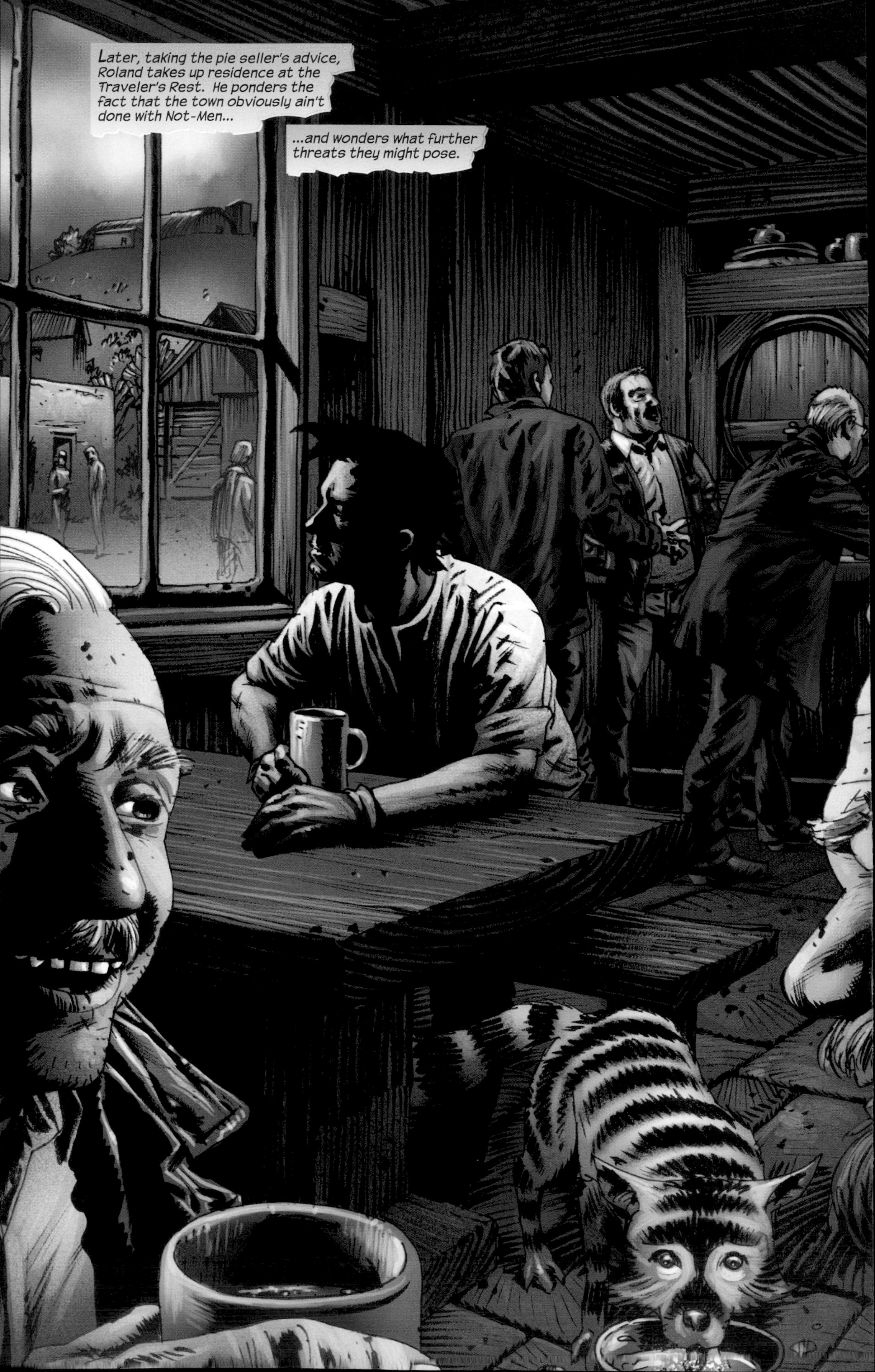
Later, taking the pie seller's advice, Roland takes up residence at the Traveler's Rest. He ponders the fact that the town obviously ain't done with Not-Men...
...and wonders what further threats they might pose.

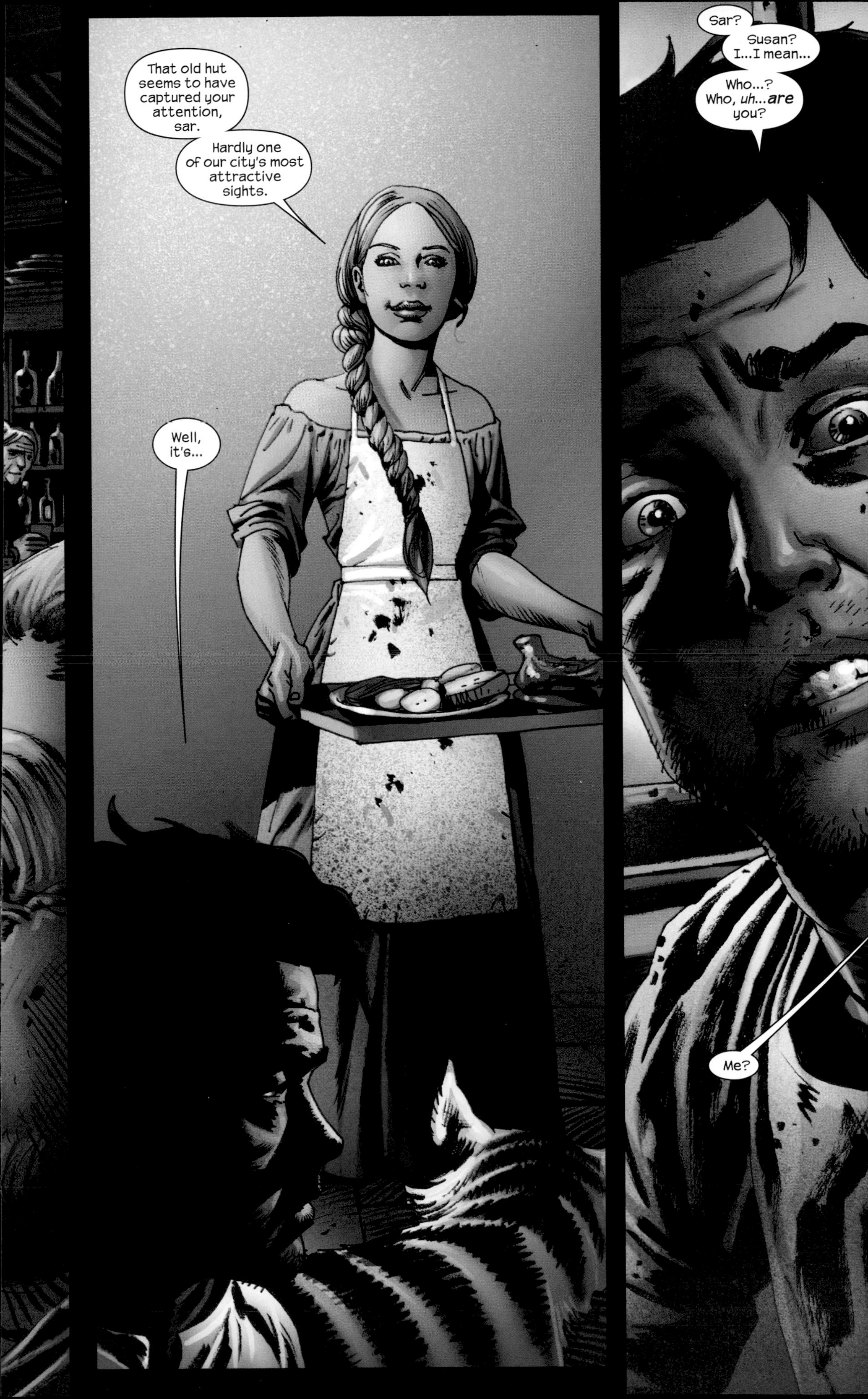
That old hut seems to have captured your attention, sar.
Hardly one of our city's most attractive sights.
Well, it's...
Sar?
Susan? I...I mean...
Who...? Who, *uh*...***are*** you?
Me?

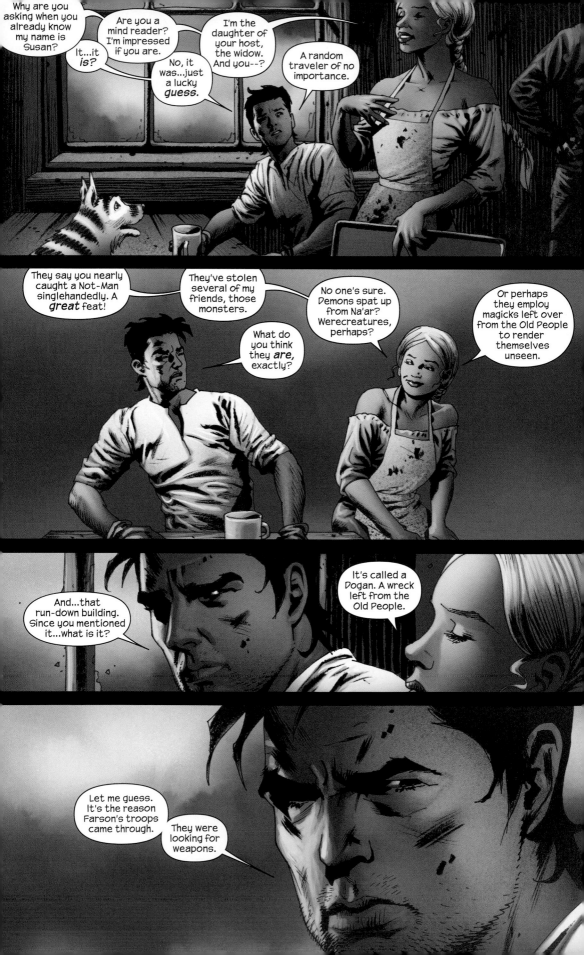

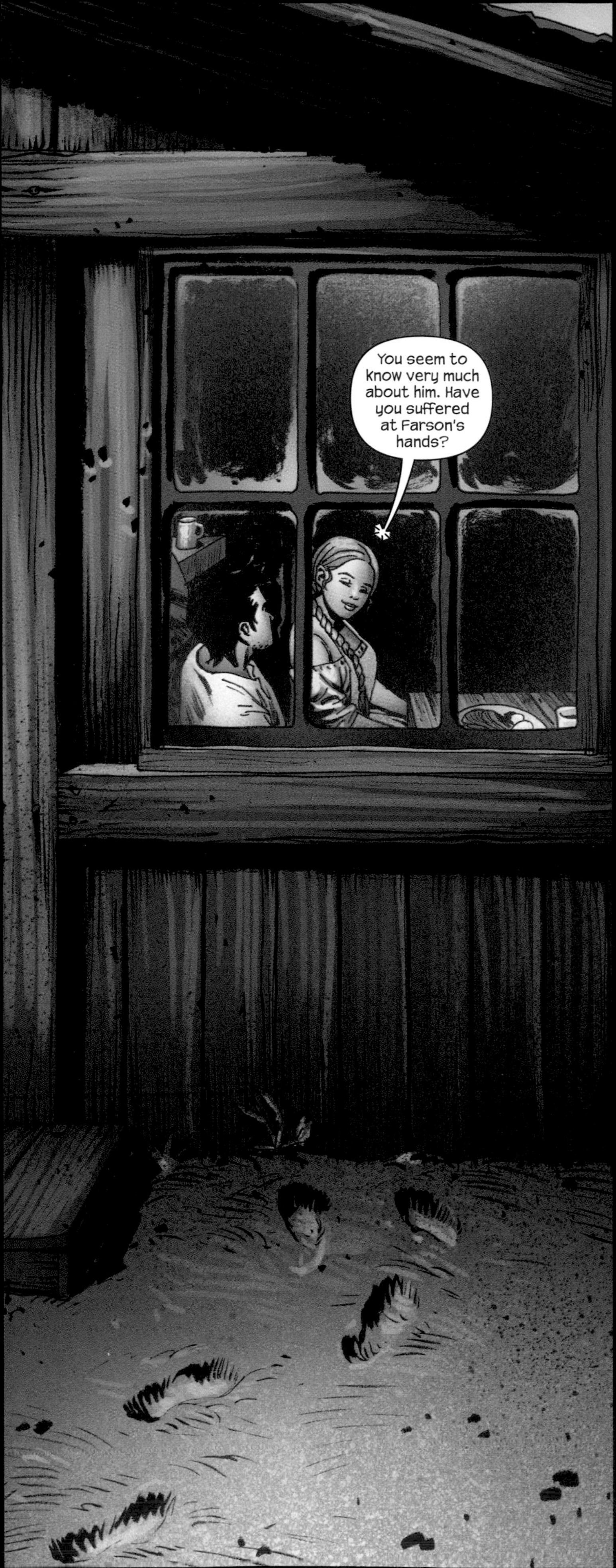
You seem to know very much about him. Have you suffered at Farson's hands?

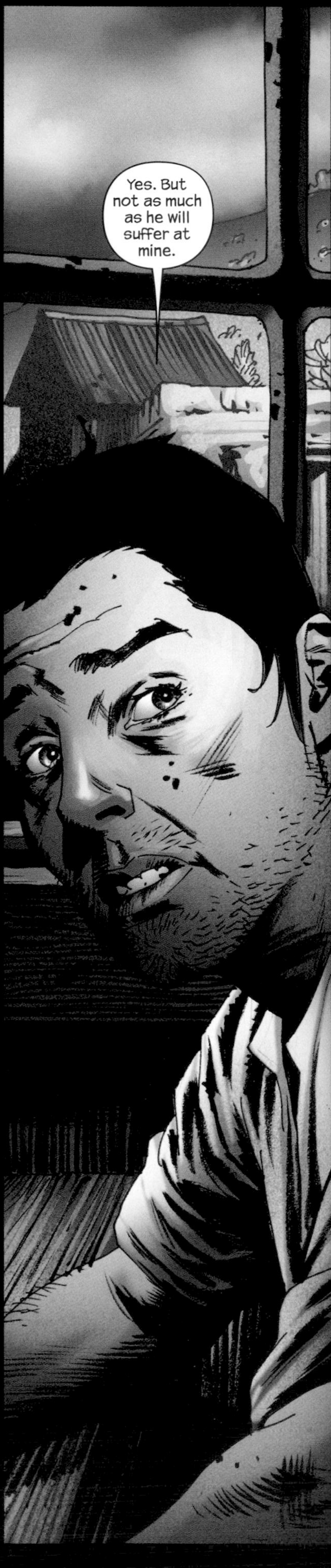
Yes. But not as much as he will suffer at mine.

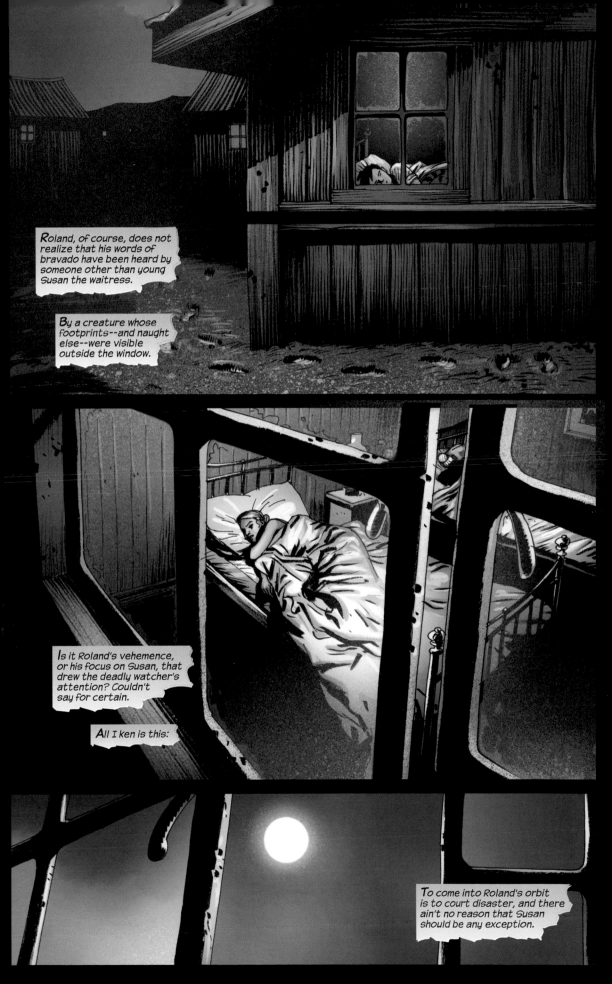

Roland, of course, does not realize that his words of bravado have been heard by someone other than young Susan the waitress.

By a creature whose footprints--and naught else--were visible outside the window.

Is it Roland's vehemence, or his focus on Susan, that drew the deadly watcher's attention? Couldn't say for certain.

All I ken is this:

To come into Roland's orbit is to court disaster, and there ain't no reason that Susan should be any exception.

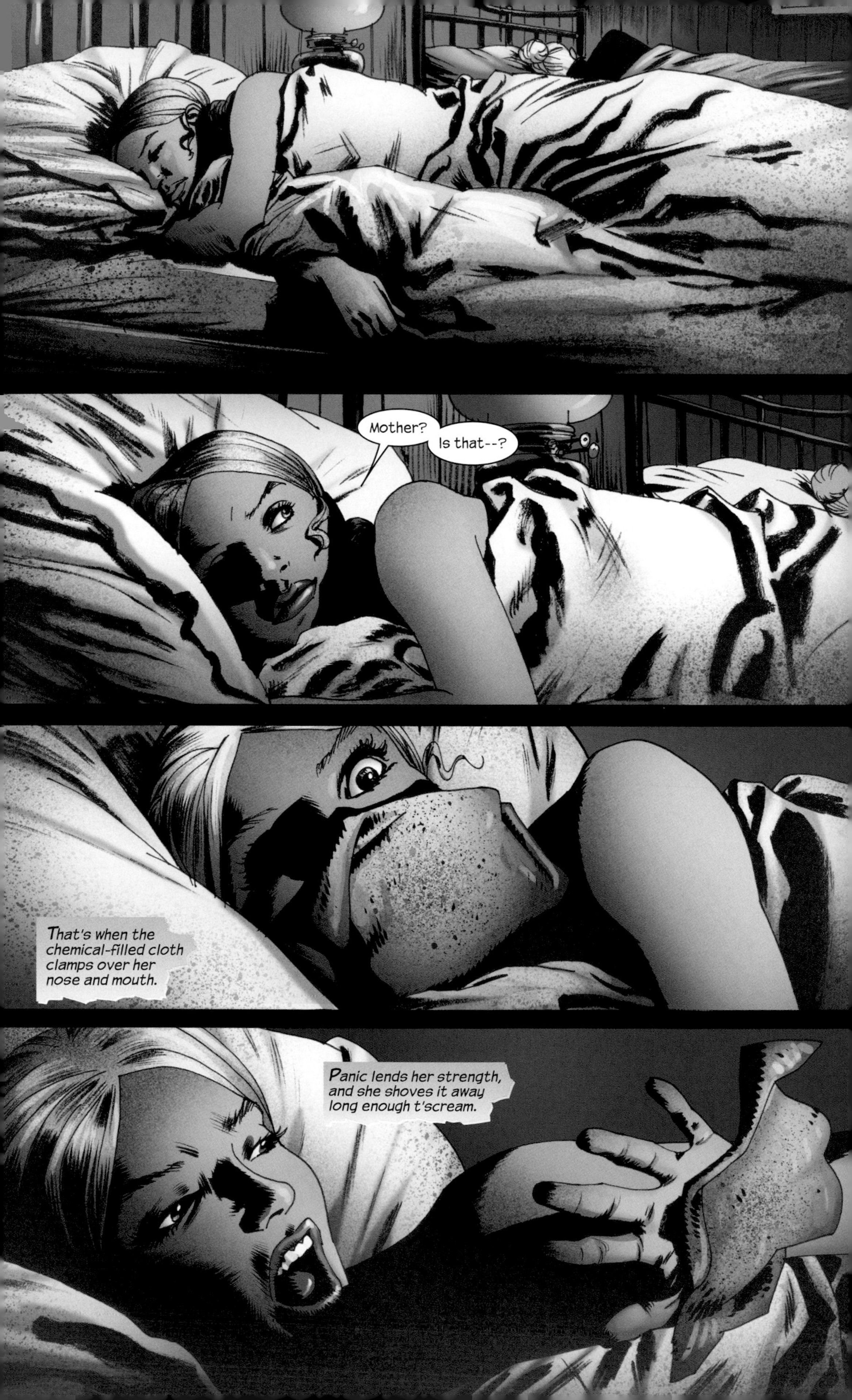
Mother?
Is that--?
That's when the chemical-filled cloth clamps over her nose and mouth.
Panic lends her strength, and she shoves it away long enough t'scream.

STEPHEN KING

THE DARK TOWER
~ THE GUNSLINGER ~

THE JOURNEY BEGINS
CHAPTER FIVE

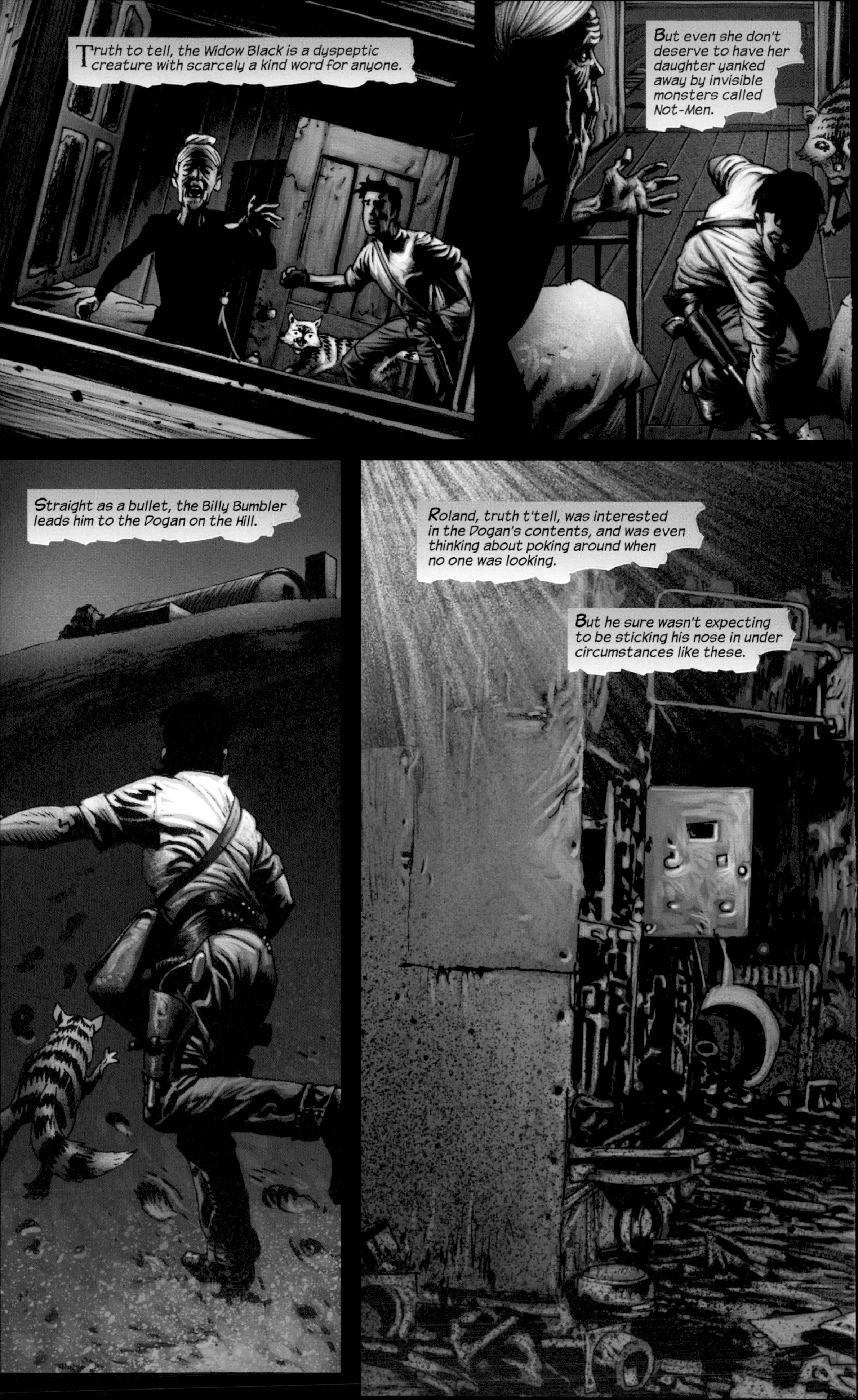
Truth to tell, the Widow Black is a dyspeptic creature with scarcely a kind word for anyone.
But even she don't deserve to have her daughter yanked away by invisible monsters called Not-Men.
Straight as a bullet, the Billy Bumbler leads him to the Dogan on the Hill.
Roland, truth t'tell, was interested in the Dogan's contents, and was even thinking about poking around when no one was looking.
But he sure wasn't expecting to be sticking his nose in under circumstances like these.

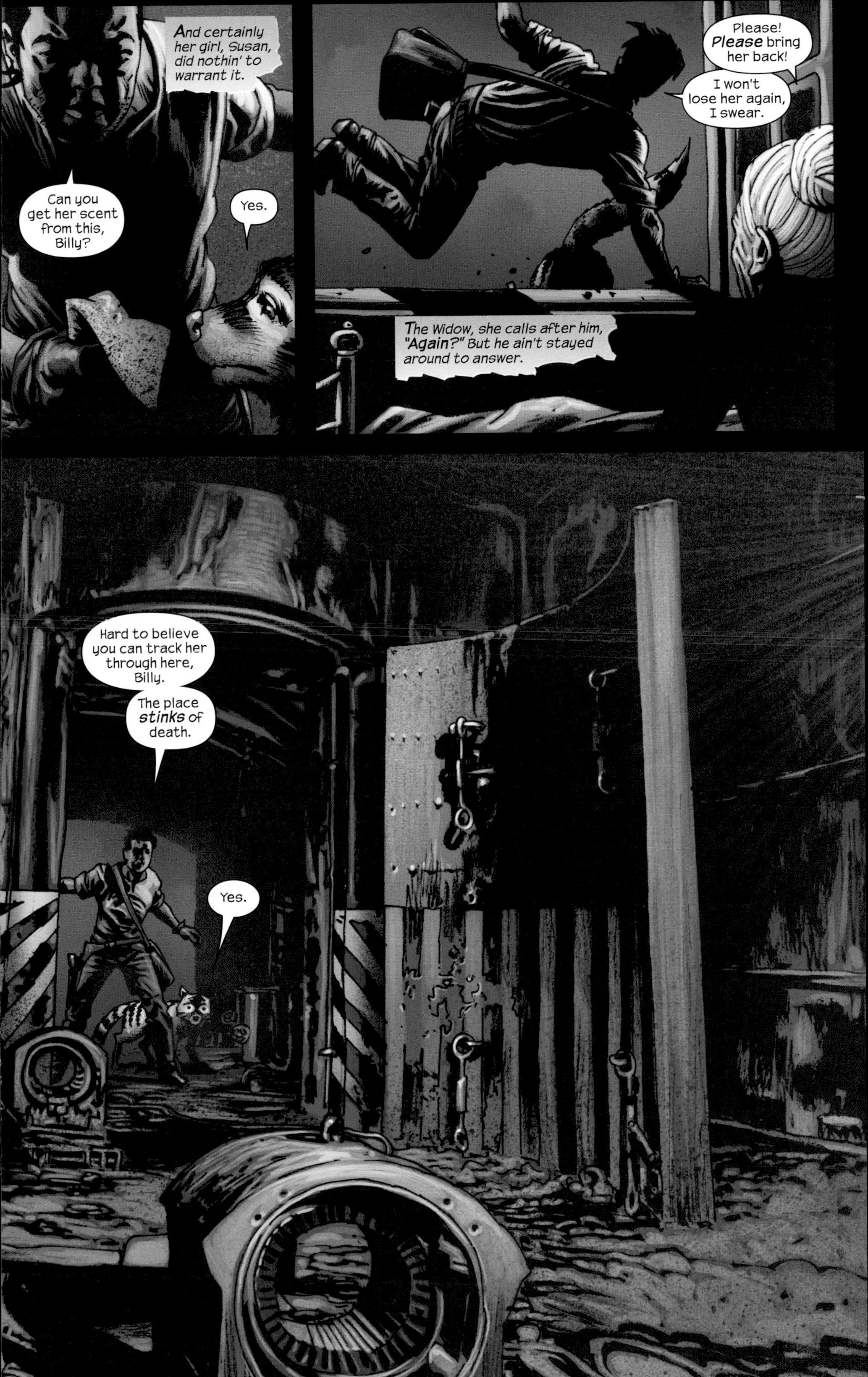

And certainly her girl, Susan, did nothin' to warrant it.
Can you get her scent from this, Billy?
Yes.
Please! Please bring her back!
I won't lose her again, I swear.
The Widow, she calls after him, "Again?" But he ain't stayed around to answer.
Hard to believe you can track her through here, Billy.
The place stinks of death.
Yes.

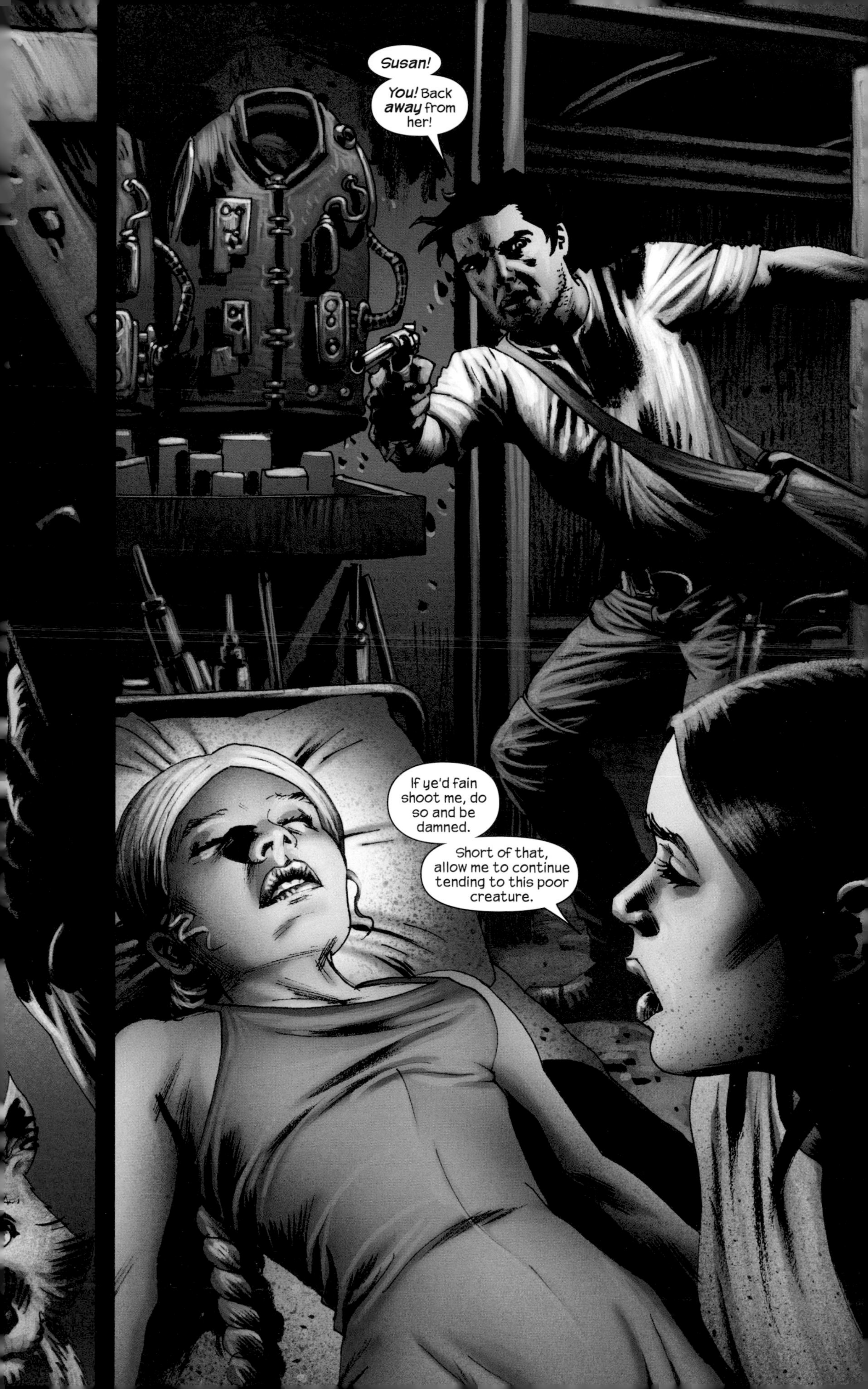
Susan!
You! Back away from her!
If ye'd fain shoot me, do so and be damned.
Short of that, allow me to continue tending to this poor creature.

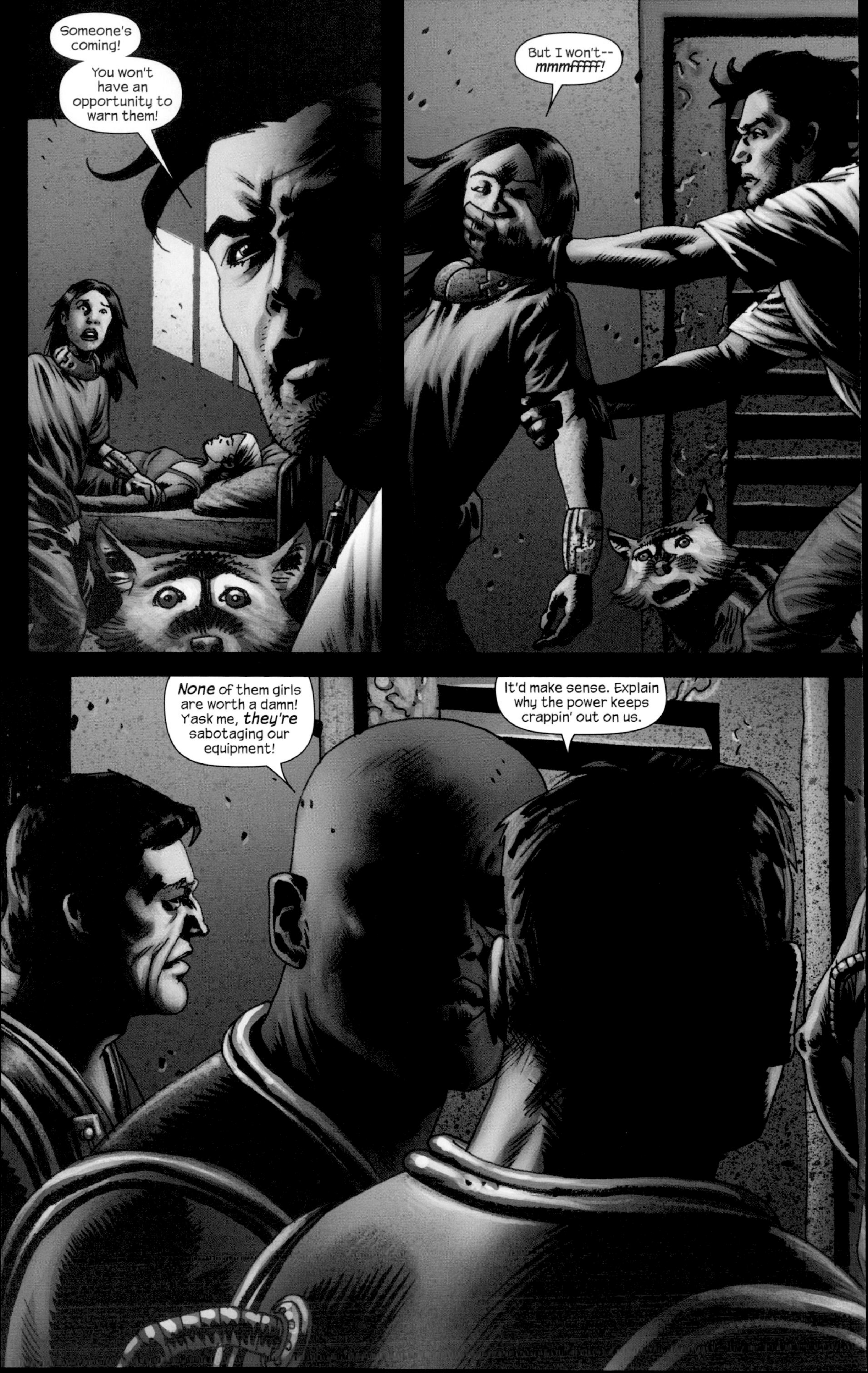
Someone's coming!
You won't have an opportunity to warn them!
But I won't-- *mmmffffff!*
None of them girls are worth a damn! Y'ask me, ***they're*** sabotaging our equipment!
It'd make sense. Explain why the power keeps crappin' out on us.

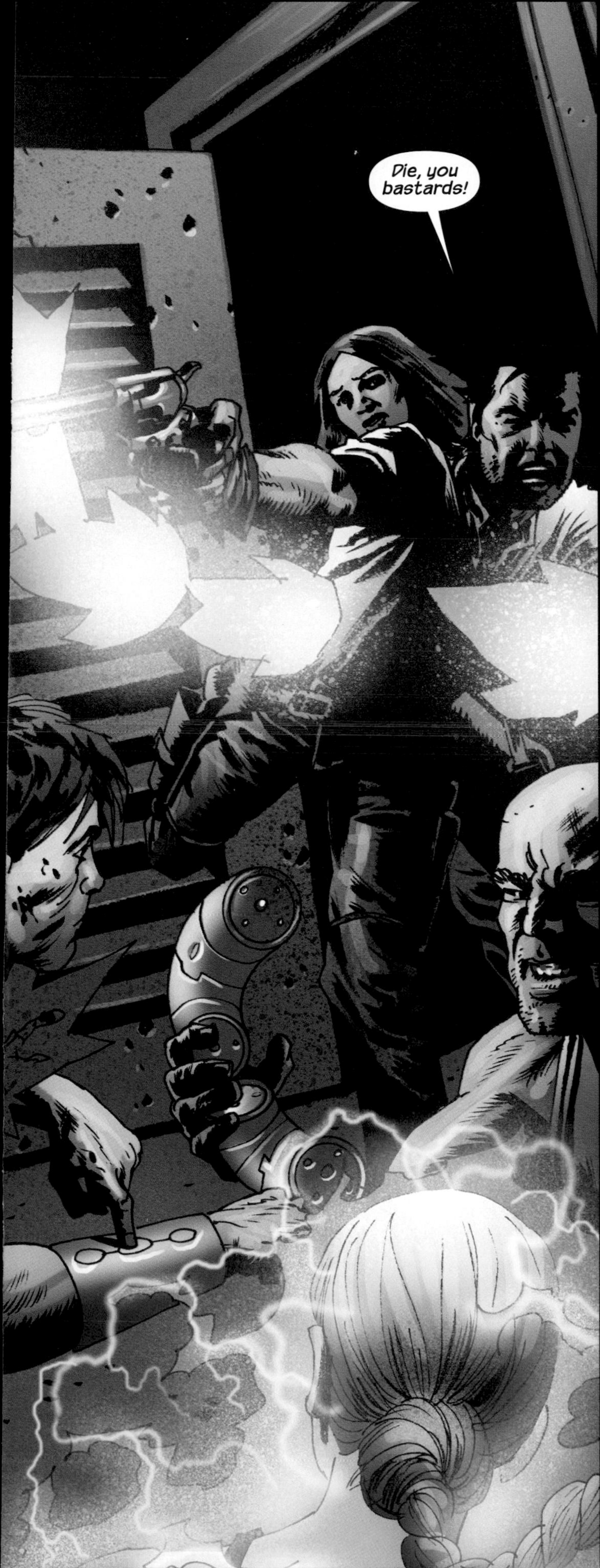
Die, you bastards!

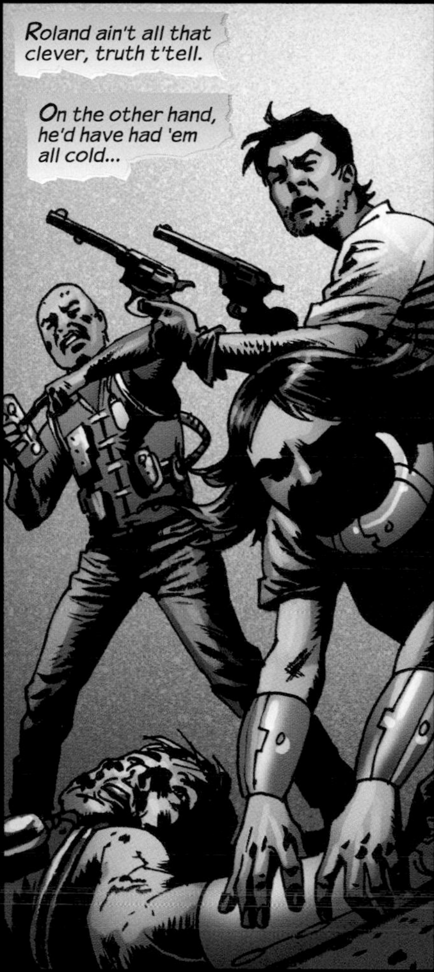
Roland ain't all that clever, truth t'tell.
On the other hand, he'd have had 'em all cold...

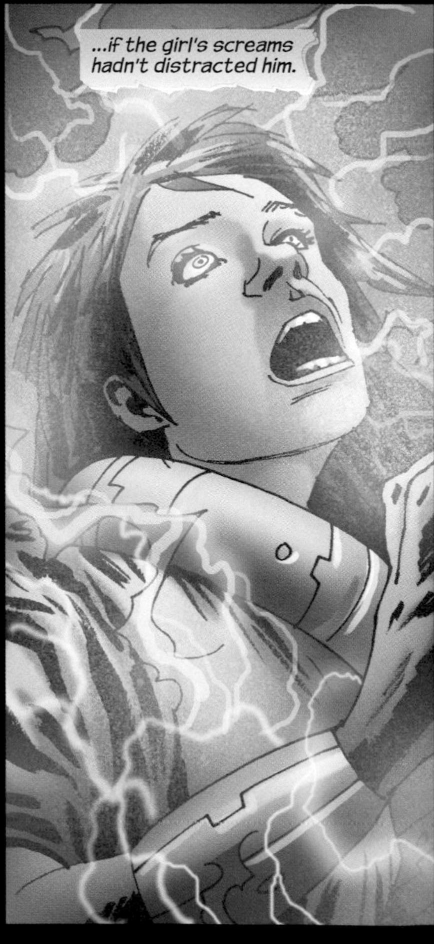
...if the girl's screams hadn't distracted him.

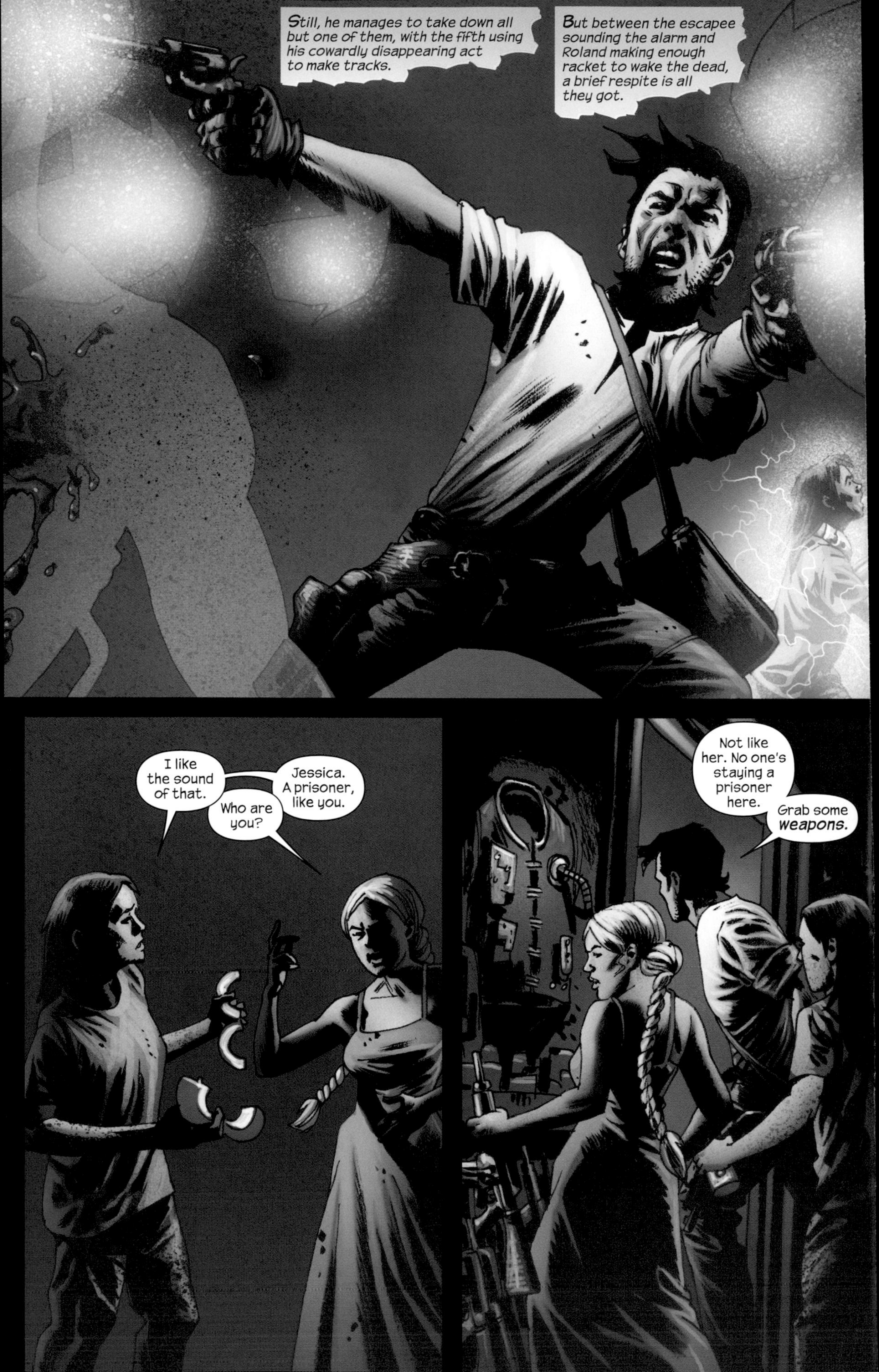
Still, he manages to take down all but one of them, with the fifth using his cowardly disappearing act to make tracks.
But between the escapee sounding the alarm and Roland making enough racket to wake the dead, a brief respite is all they got.
Who are you?
Jessica. A prisoner, like you.
I like the sound of that.
Not like her. No one's staying a prisoner here.
Grab some weapons.

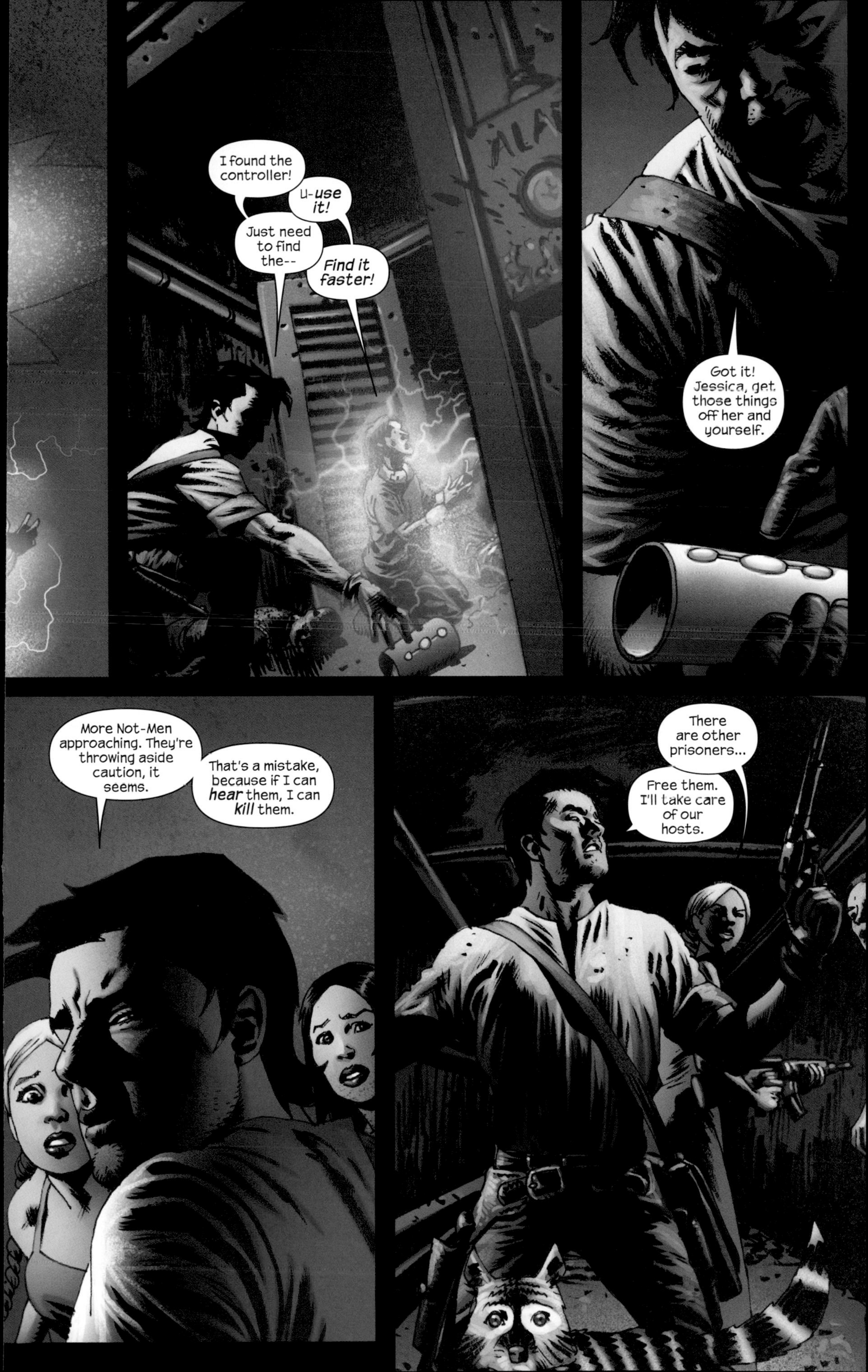
I found the controller!
U-use it!
Just need to find the--
Find it faster!
Got it! Jessica, get those things off her and yourself.
More Not-Men approaching. They're throwing aside caution, it seems.
That's a mistake, because if I can hear them, I can kill them.
There are other prisoners...
Free them. I'll take care of our hosts.

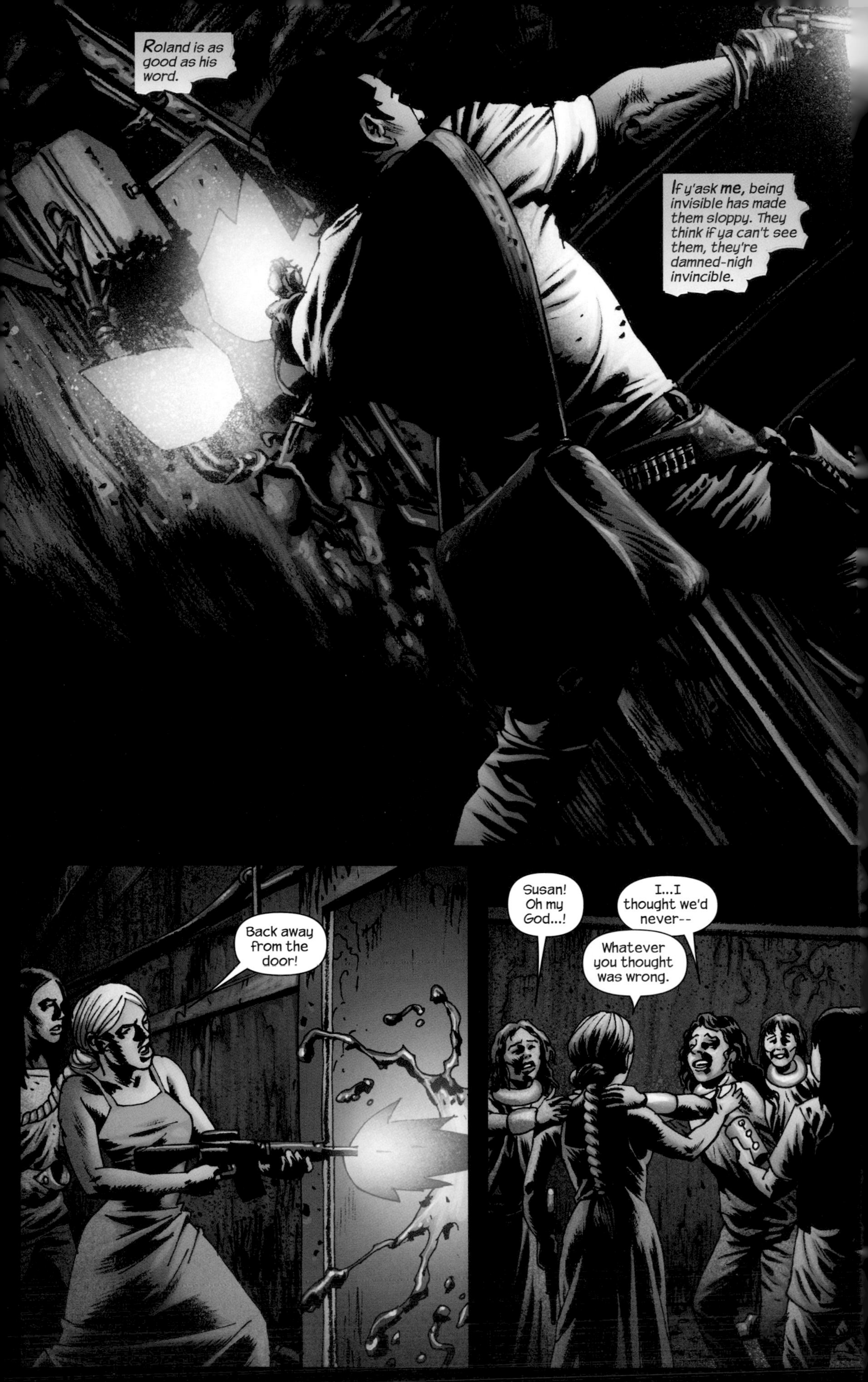
Roland is as good as his word.
If y'ask me, being invisible has made them sloppy. They think if ya can't see them, they're damned-nigh invincible.
Back away from the door!
Susan! Oh my God...!
I...I thought we'd never--
Whatever you thought was wrong.

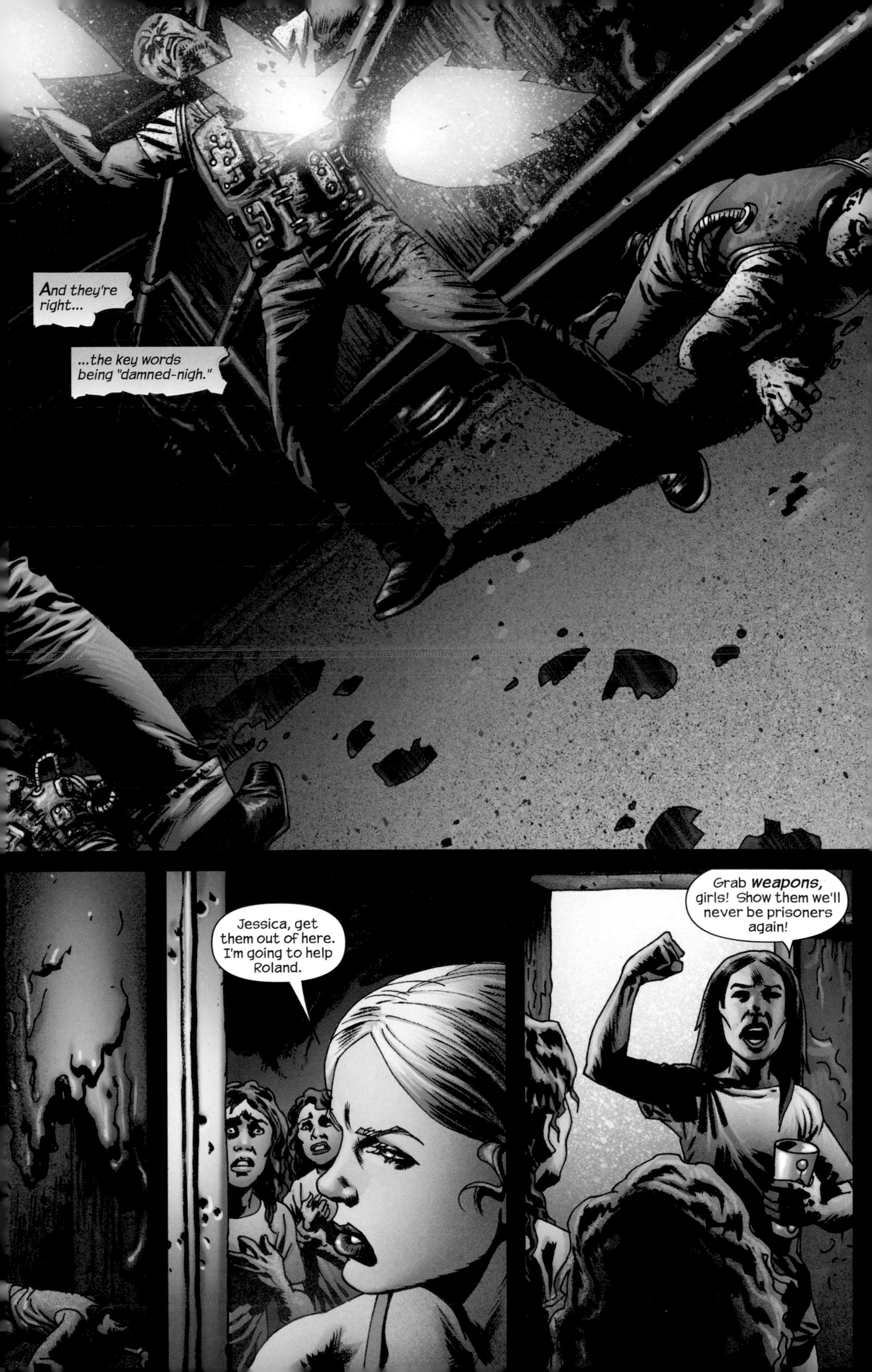
And they're right...
...the key words being "damned-nigh."
Jessica, get them out of here. I'm going to help Roland.
Grab weapons, girls! Show them we'll never be prisoners again!

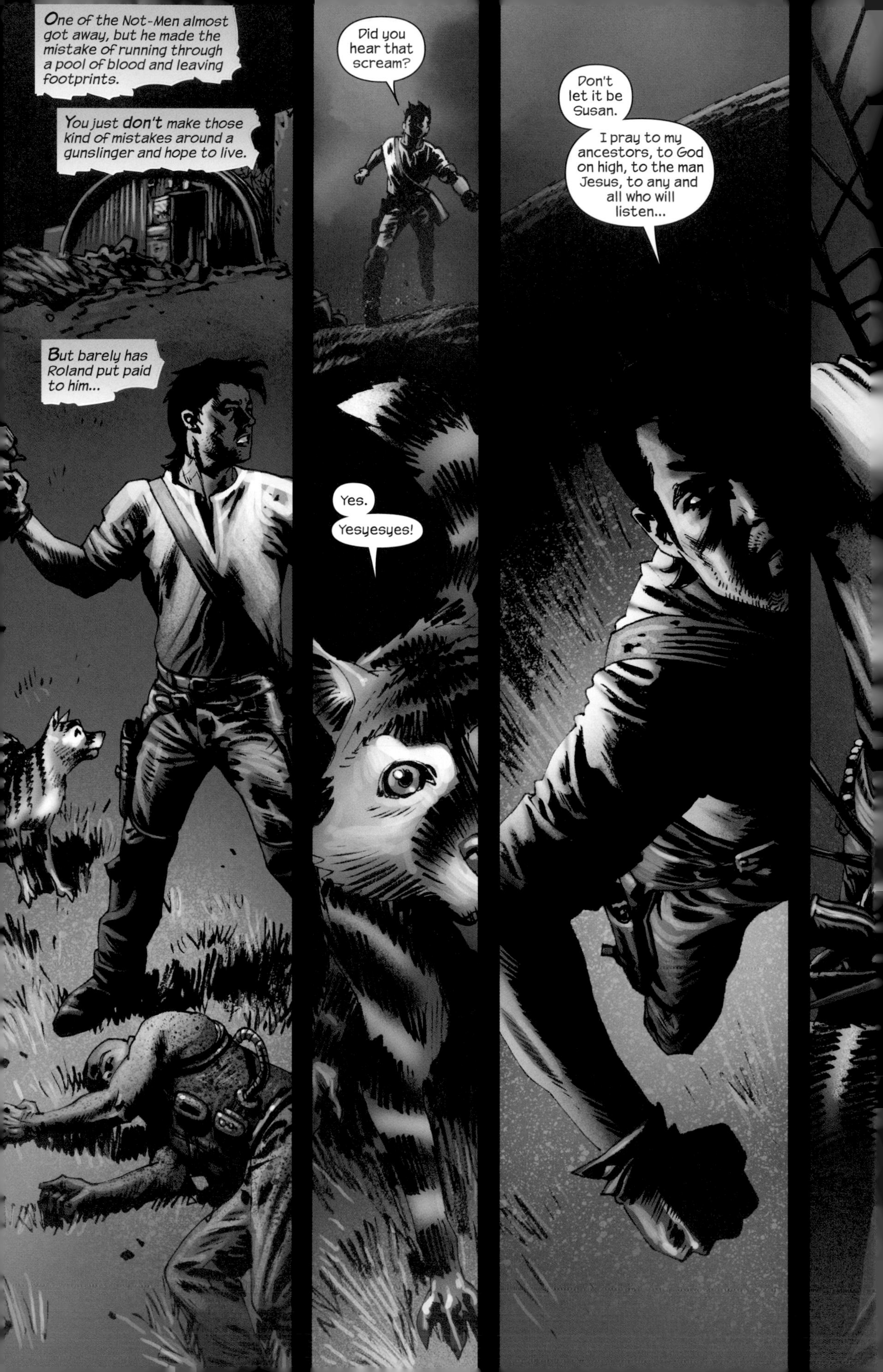

One of the Not-Men almost got away, but he made the mistake of running through a pool of blood and leaving footprints.
You just don't make those kind of mistakes around a gunslinger and hope to live.
But barely has Roland put paid to him...
Did you hear that scream?
Yes.
Yesyesyes!
Don't let it be Susan.
I pray to my ancestors, to God on high, to the man Jesus, to any and all who will listen...

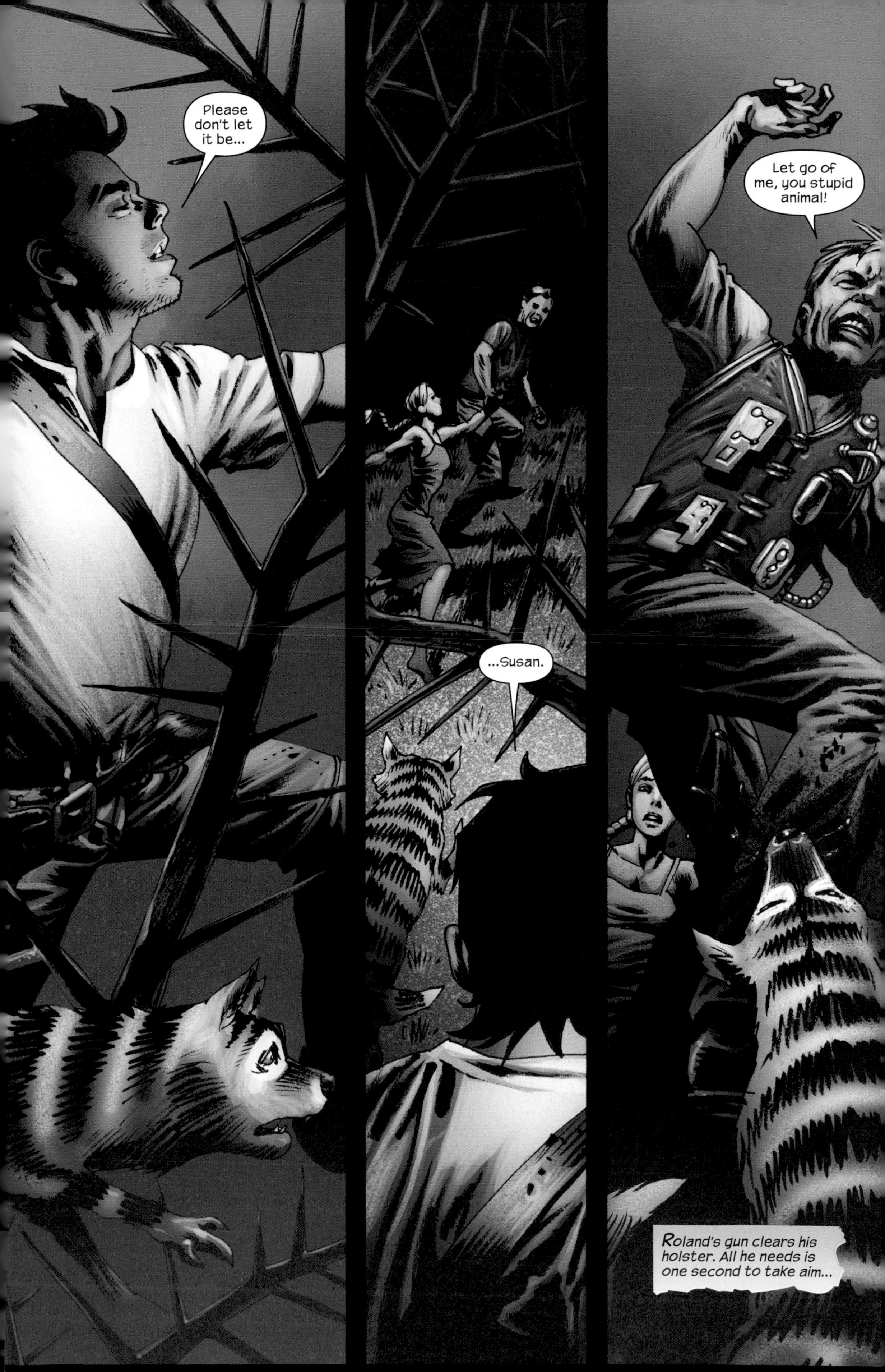
Please don't let it be...
...Susan.
Let go of me, you stupid animal!
Roland's gun clears his holster. All he needs is one second to take aim...

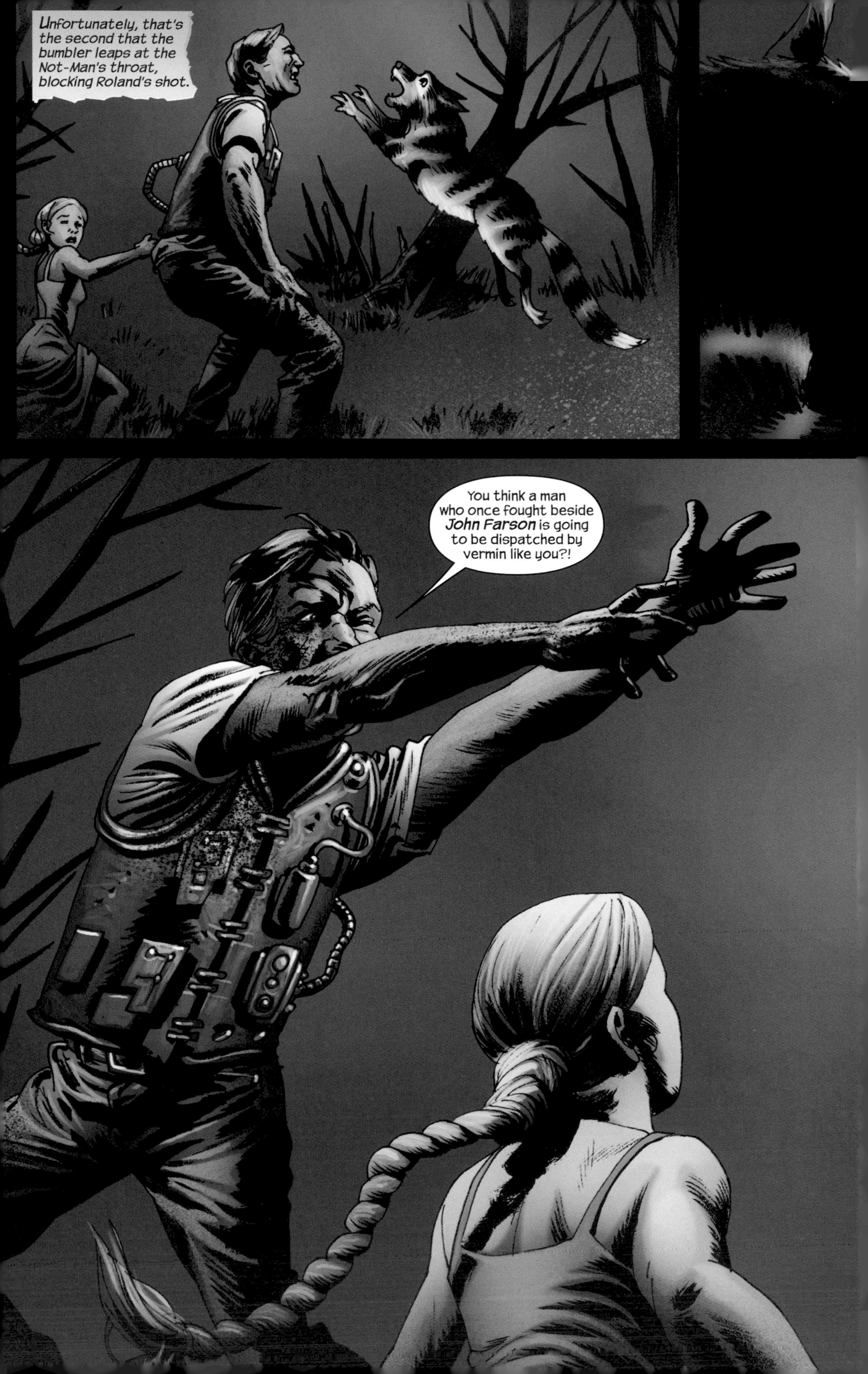
Unfortunately, that's the second that the bumbler leaps at the Not-Man's throat, blocking Roland's shot.
You think a man who once fought beside John Farson is going to be dispatched by vermin like you?!

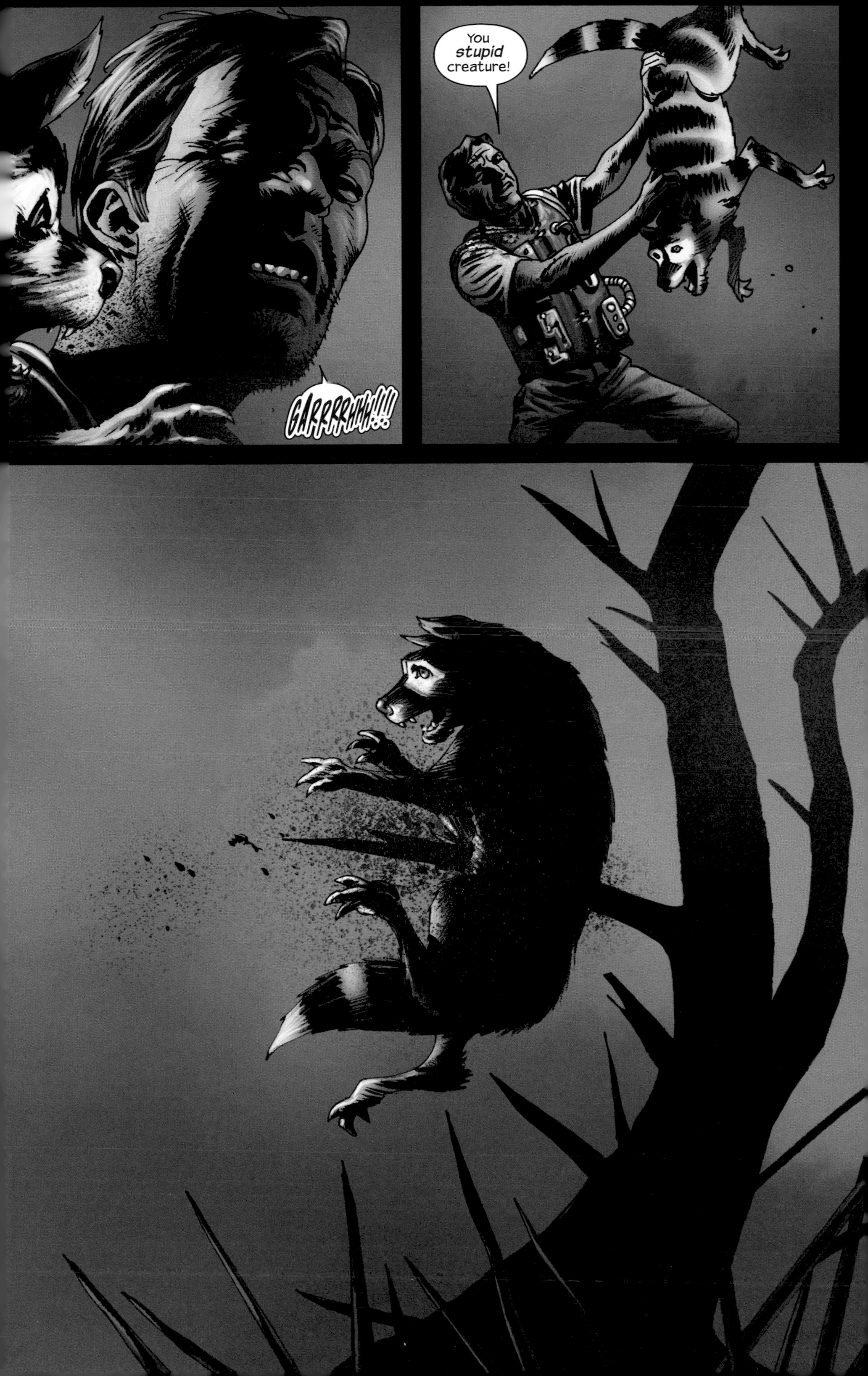
GARRRRHHH!!!
You *stupid* creature!

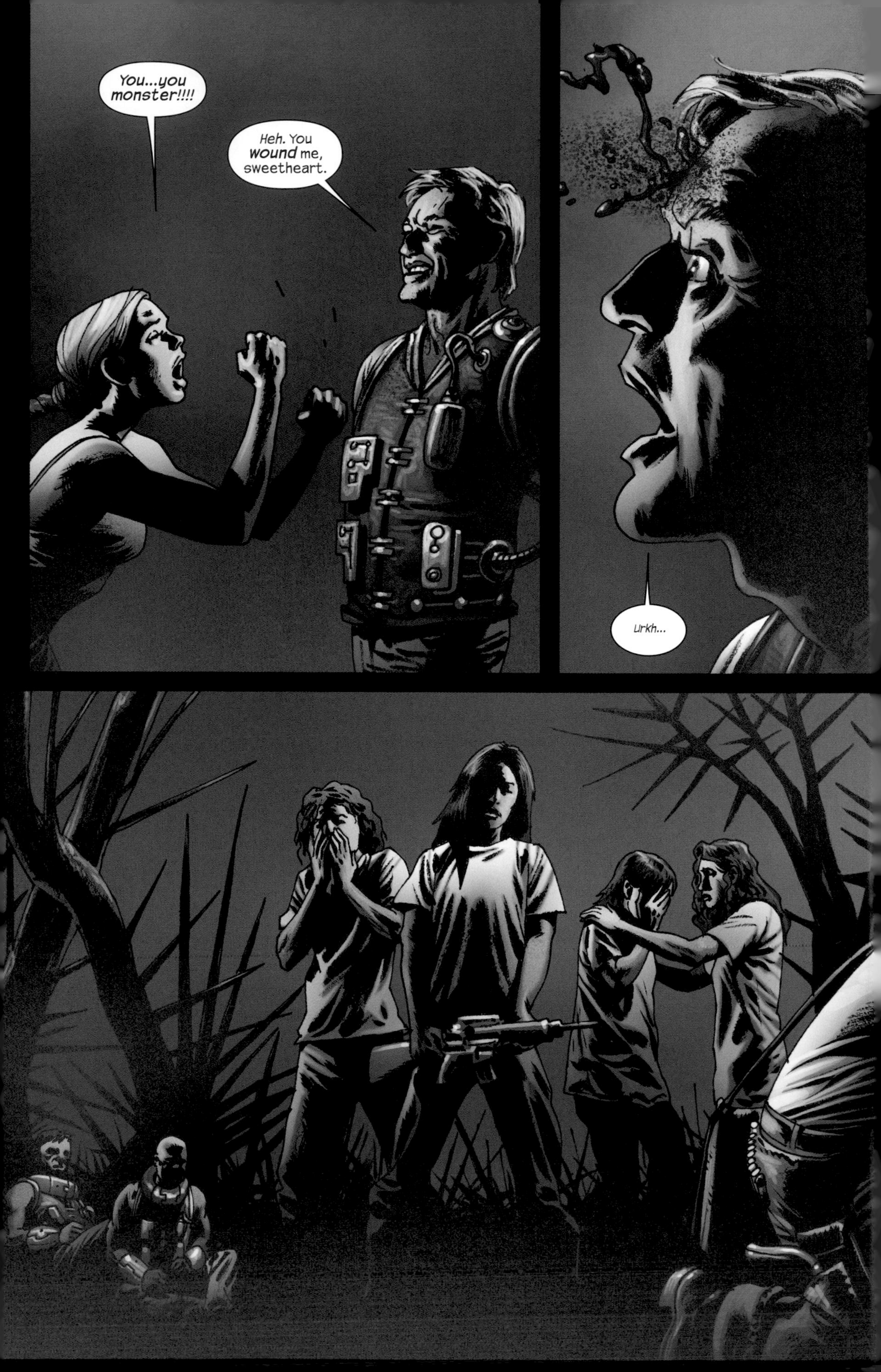
You...you monster!!!!
Heh. You wound me, sweetheart.
Urkh...

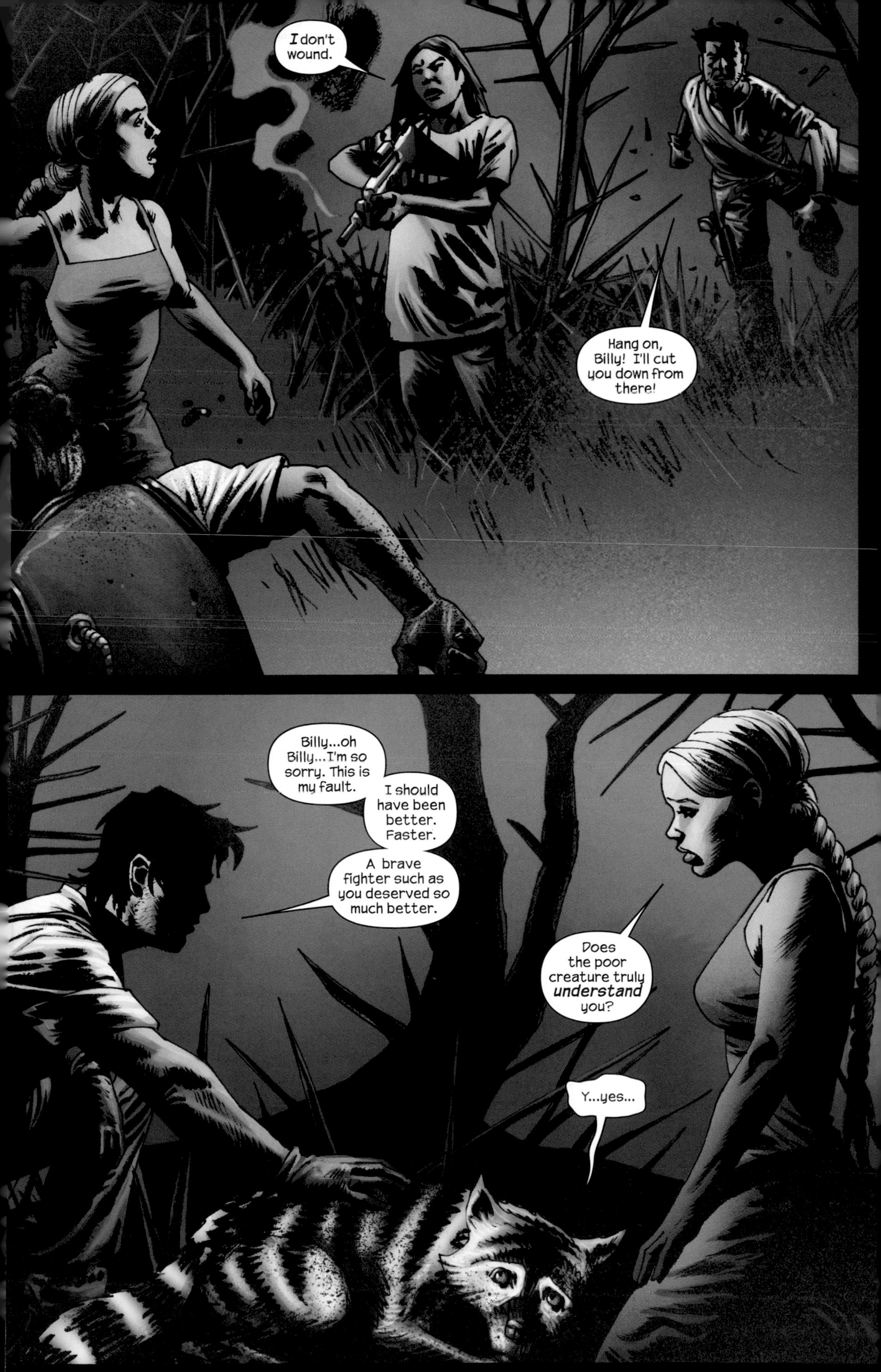
I don't wound.
Hang on, Billy! I'll cut you down from there!
Billy...oh Billy...I'm so sorry. This is my fault.
I should have been better. Faster.
A brave fighter such as you deserved so much better.
Does the poor creature truly understand you?
Y...yes...

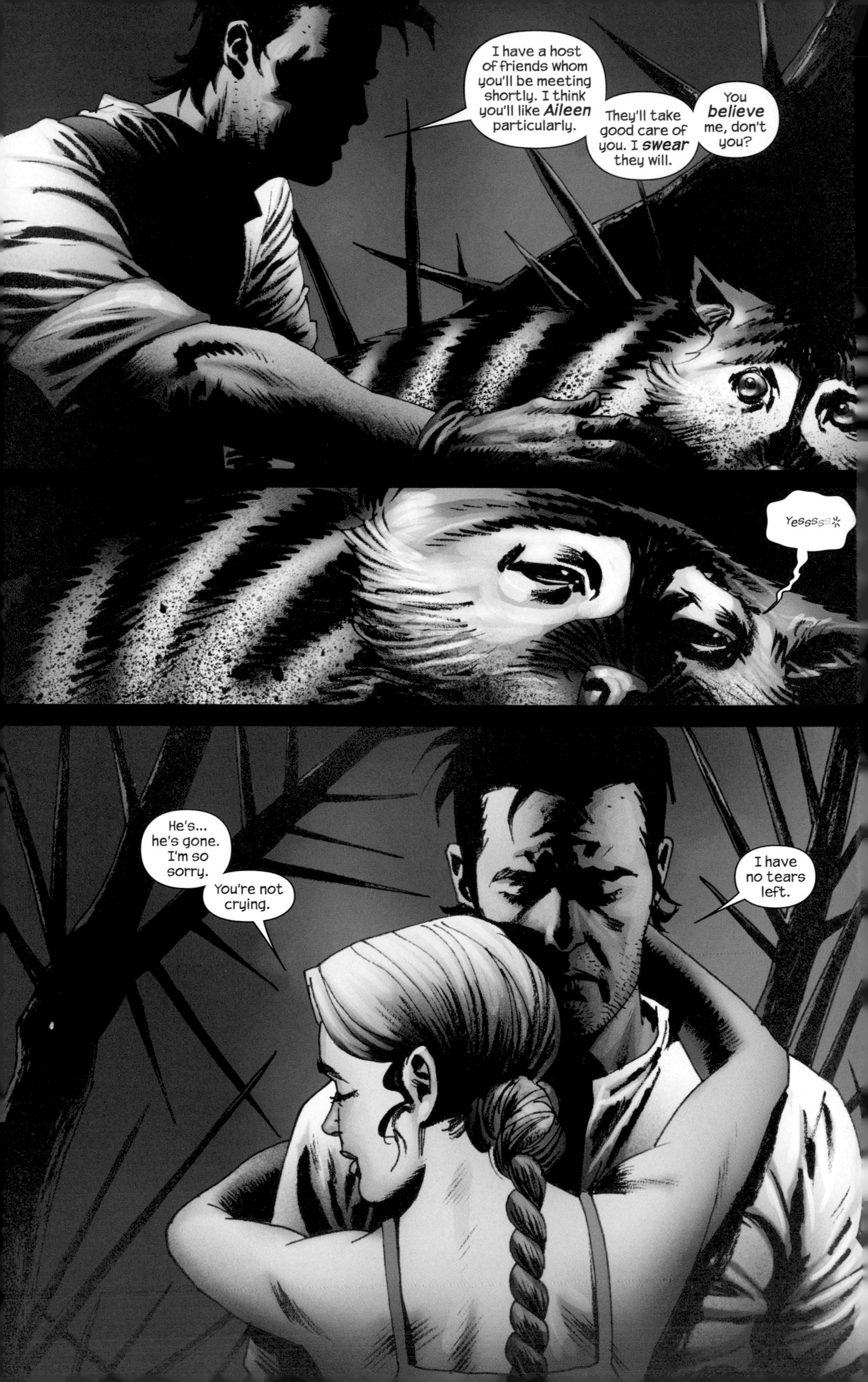
I have a host of friends whom you'll be meeting shortly. I think you'll like *Aileen* particularly.
They'll take good care of you. I *swear* they will.
You *believe* me, don't you?
Yessss
He's... he's gone. I'm so sorry.
You're not crying.
I have no tears left.

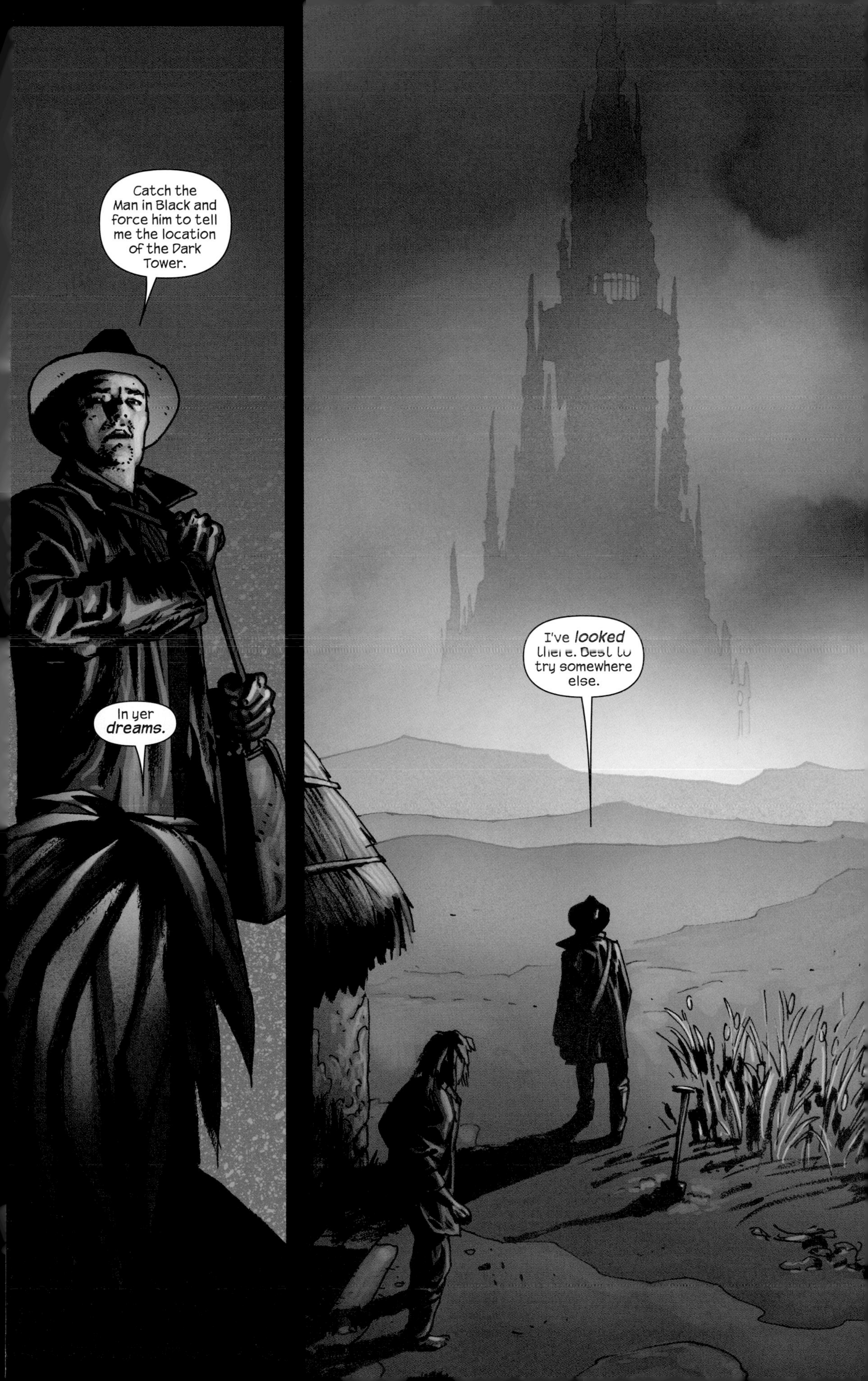
Catch the Man in Black and force him to tell me the location of the Dark Tower.
In yer *dreams.*
I've *looked* there. Best to try somewhere else.

ACKNOWLEDGMENTS

Grateful acknowledgments to the following at Marvel Comics for
their invaluable contributions in expanding The Dark Tower universe:
Ralph Macchio, Anthony Dial, Irene Y. Lee, Jeff Powell, Taylor Esposito,
Michael Horwitz, Mark D. Beazley, Nelson Ribeiro, Alex Starbuck,
Jennifer Grunwald, Jeff Youngquist, David Gabriel, Michael Pasciullo,
Ruwan Jayatilleke, Spring Hoteling, Patrick McGrath, Alex Alonso,
Joe Quesada, and Dan Buckley.

Special thanks to Chuck Verrill, Marsha DeFilipo,
Chris Lotts, Barbara Ann McIntyre, Brian Stark, Jim Nausedas,
Jim McCann, Arune Singh, Jeff Suter, John Barber,
Lauren Sankovitch, and Chris Eliopoulos.

THE EPIC SAGA
CONTINUES IN...
THE GUNSLINGER

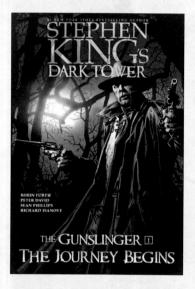

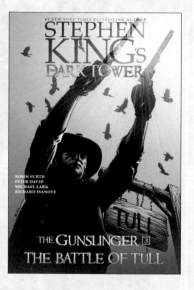

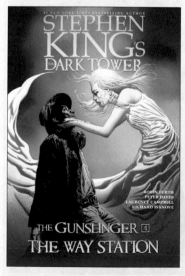

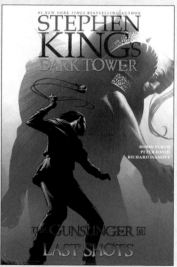

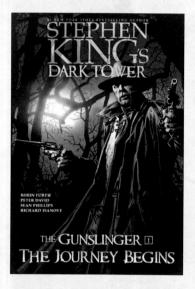

Available from

GALLERY 13
An Imprint of Simon & Schuster
A CBS COMPANY

Also available in
THE DARK TOWER
graphic novel series
BEGINNINGS

Available from

GALLERY 13
An Imprint of Simon & Schuster
A CBS COMPANY

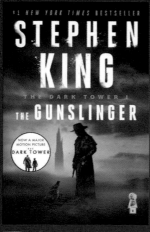
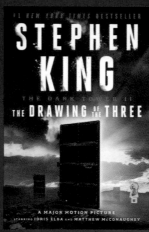
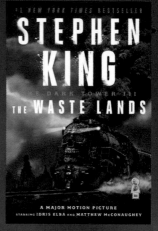
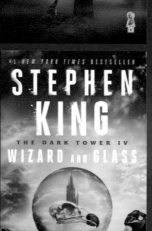
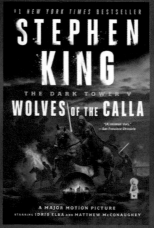

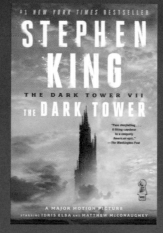

63735